GOOD NEWS IN
THE EARLY CHURCH

GOOD NEWS IN
THE EARLY CHURCH

1 & 2 Timothy, Titus, James,
1 & 2 Peter, 1, 2 & 3 John and *Jude*
in Today's English Version

introduced by
MARTIN E. MARTY

Collins
Fontana Books

in co-operation with The Bible Reading Fellowship

First published in Fontana Books 1976
© Martin E. Marty 1976

Today's English Version of *1 & 2 Timothy, Titus, James,
1 & 2 Peter, 1, 2 & 3 John* and *Jude*
© American Bible Society, New York, 1966, 1971

Made and printed in Great Britain by
William Collins Sons & Co Ltd Glasgow

TO THE MEMORY OF
PAUL M. BRETSCHER
WHO INTRODUCED ME TO
NEW TESTAMENT STUDIES

CONTENTS

PREFACE

'That's not my period.' Many a historian can avoid comment on a technical point by using such a phrase. If I am a specialist on the fifteenth century, do not hold me responsible for knowledge of events in the fourteenth. When the invitation came to this 'Professor of the History of Modern Christianity', as my title has it, to introduce *Good News in the Early Church*, a simple evasion could have been, 'That's not my period.' But no historian of Christianity and no Christian in general can really say of the latter decades of the first Christian century, 'That's not my period.'

The time when the apostles were transmitting their witness and inheritance, when the New Testament Scriptures were taking shape, and when the faith was being spread throughout the Roman Empire is never left behind. In a sense it 'genetically programmes' the later Church, both anticipating later development and providing reference points for it. Today's issues of life and work, faith and order can rarely be addressed without knowledge of this period.

Beyond this point of substance, personal reasons also made the invitation attractive. Return to the New Testament and the early Church was a return to a first love. My baccalaureate days in theological studies focused on the study of Greek, the New Testament, and early Christian literature. The factors that lured me in Master's studies to the Reformation and, on the doctoral and vocational levels, to the modern period, are elusive, complicated, and beside the point here. Suffice it to say that the year of study spent preparing this introduction was a time of great enjoyment, the recall of a past that I cherish and the living with a promise that few Christians have failed to find in these documents.

This book takes up 'all those little books at the end of the Bible', save for the one-chapter Pauline Letter to Philemon. It also reserves for others the two *big* books at the end, the Letter to the Hebrews and Revelation. The pastoral letters and the letters of James, Peter, John, and Jude are less well known than the gospels or the Pauline epistles. Some of them, particularly 2 Peter and Jude and parts of the pastorals will not impress readers in the same ways other parts of the Bible will, though 2 Timothy, 1 Peter, and 1 John in particular have passages that rank with the best of the Good News in Scripture. Even where they are less attractive and compelling, however, these letters deserve interest as almost the only surviving glimpses of life and thought in several crucial decades of church history.

I make two pleas to readers. The first, addressed to technical scholars, is made or implied by all introducers in this series. Remember that this is not a word-for-word or line-by-line commentary on the original text. The libraries have many such books; they are attractive to leaders and professional students; I have consulted the more substantial of these throughout. In the nature of the case and because of the demands of the format, it was not always possible to give full credit to the source of each interpretation.

The second plea, to the two halves of a presumed readership, asks them to be patient with each other, with the scholars who probe the historical and literary contexts, and with me as a fellow-reader and transmitter. I speak of two halves because it is easy to picture readership almost equally divided into two groups. One group of faithful and generally conservative readers instinctively holds to the traditional authorship and early dating of all these letters. For them, these are by the apostle Paul; James, Jesus' brother; the apostle Peter; the apostle and beloved disciple John; someone named Jude, the brother of James. The names of these authors do not always even appear in the texts, but they have long been associated with, or for other reasons they can be linked with, these apostolic figures. To call these ties into question would be to doubt the veracity of the Scriptures and to deny their authority, in the minds of some.

In reading for this introduction I took pains to revisit the comments of those who are called conservative Catholics and evangelicals. I came to have renewed respect for their devotion to Scripture and their scholarly sophistication, even if now and then their efforts to 'make things come out right' seemed so strenuous that it raised suspicions about the validity of that part of their enterprise. Many of them make a good case for traditional views or for the reasons for holding to them. Many of their contentions are upheld by some scholars who do not completely agree with them or who do not feel constrained for theological reasons to hold to the conventional attributions of authorship. At times one feels that their insistences do blind them to some of the excitements of early Christian formation and to some enduring problems. But I found them unattractive only when they claimed monopolies on truth and virtue, or when they accused others in 'the other camp' of stupidity or bad faith.

The other camp is the very broad self-critical community of scholars who find no *a priori* theological reasons for holding to early dates or traditional apostolic authorship. They do not all agree with each other. They see no reason to agree in all details and find no basis for such concord. Some of the problems of authorship do seem insoluble. Many an hour I spent comparing differing approaches and then asking myself, with ever more sense of personal involvement: 'Now, what do you think? What is really the case?' Yet I could not always come up with satisfying answers.

What impressed me about the members of this fellowship of critical scholars was their ability to convey the sense of how the Church took shape, of the day-to-day struggles of Christian people and especially of their leaders. Almost always their respect for biblical authority marked their efforts; not a few of them clearly were interested in getting out of the way of the Good News, letting it speak. One hesitates to speak of a middle ground between the two groups, but there are at least vague outlines of dim shadows of a broad consensus among those critical scholars who have been respectful of tradition.

The pastoral epistles (to Timothy and Titus), a few of them say, may actually have come from the hand of Paul's 'amanuensis' or secretary and thus really from Paul, but are more likely a stringing together of authentic Pauline material prepared for people in a later situation. James may be a leader who seems to have had great authority in Jerusalem, and who could have been Jesus' brother, though some problems result if one accepts this view. Those who try to do justice to Petrine authorship think that the Silvanus mentioned in 1 Peter was the true editor and collator of Peter's expressions. Almost none feel that 2 Peter or Jude could be anything but very late writings, certainly from decades after Peter and his contemporaries were dead. Have a clear conscience, timid readers: from the first these were 'spoken against' books, uncertainly located in the biblical canon. Doubts about them were raised by Luther and Calvin and other assured 'mainstream' Christians who had the highest views of biblical authority. Finally, the letters from John are usually attributed by this wing of the critical camp to the author of the Fourth Gospel. They see him as probably an Ephesian elder named John, one who was close to the drama of earliest Christian witness.

Only where questions of authorship bear on interpretation will these issues be addressed. They will not become major preoccupations. In the act of pleading that they do not become obsessive it may be that I have

only succeeded in placing them higher on my readers'
agenda than they should be. I write in the confidence that
today's Christians at the very least like to be apprised of the
issues of biblical interpretation, and that both they and
those readers to whom the Bible does not come as the
Good News for their lives will enjoy and profit from even
the most brief attempts to reconstruct details of life in
the earliest Christian decades.

THE PASTORAL LETTERS: TO TIMOTHY AND TITUS

For the best of news, readers of the Bible might turn to the book of Isaiah the prophet, or to the gospels of Luke and John. To hear the news interpreted, they would read Paul's Letter to the Romans. In these books people witness the mighty deeds of God. The drama of his saving ways is often full of wonder and suspense. Men and women respond with full commitment or agonize in the reaches of their souls. Faith is then an incandescent incident. People die for it, or live in the presence of Jesus Christ the Risen One.

Not all of life is lived in terms of such thrill or decision. At times these central scriptural writings offer almost more than later strugglers can bear. They then feel that they suffer by contrast. Why does no temple vision happen to me? I am kept at a distance by a book in which a man walks down the road and says to a tax-collector, 'Follow me!' and the tax-collector simply follows. Either this exchange implies a fanaticism that I cannot admire or a heroism that I cannot imitate.

In the gospels, Jesus says that foxes have holes and birds of the air have nests, but the Son of Man has no place to lay his head. Few seem to let this disturb them. They leave everything behind and go from village to village, healing and teaching. No one seems to have to attend to church-offering plates or parliamentary procedure. 'Be improbable!' Jesus calls to fishermen and farmers, and they venture. 'Be mad!' shouts Paul, and sets an example for others as a fool for Christ.

The honest reader has difficulty identifying with these people and events. Envy soon turns to disappointment and boredom. What does any of this have to do with my life? I punch a time-clock and put in an eight-hour day. I attend to office affairs and go to union meetings. My Christian parish activities involve me in telephone calls, some humdrum meetings, occasional bickering, attempts to define what religion is all about, and trying to find some way to be Christian and to impart the faith and its way to my children. I live in a world of mixed loyalties, half-kept promises, and compromises. Prophets may excite or shame me, but I also need a pastor to hear me and guide me.

Good News of highest quality breaks through on hundreds of pages of Scripture. But here and there are portions that address the workaday, practical life of church people. They give us glimpses of what the early church leaders thought and what they thought was or ought to be going on. Such documents, most of them tucked in near the end of the biblical canon, portray second-generation Christianity.

Mention the second generation of any movement or religious group to a social scientist and you can expect to hear a rather predictable comment. Second generations represent true problems to anything vital. Almost as if by a law of history, one can expect in them party squabbles, vying for position, competing claims as to who is the true leader, attempts to define approved doctrines and ways of living. Loose ends have to be tied. Nothing dare be left to chance. Order and organization are on everyone's mind.

Observe any movement in action. It may be the old Bolsheviks or Third World revolutionaries, flushed with success, now busying themselves with writing constitutions or detailing doctrines. Civil rights leadership in the racially divided societies of Africa and the Americas begins with a dynamism that is soon lost after the original charismatic leaders disappear. Start a great mission hospital in Africa and expect to find the succeeding generation debating the question of valid succession to the grand doctor whose vision first set everything in motion.

Emile Durkheim suggested that religious movements begin in 'effervescence'. People gather, a fresh spirit is in the air; there is a buzz of rumour and suspense. Soon that effervescence is bottled. What had been fluid crystallizes. Earliest Christianity was effervescent. The gospels and Paul's letters make that clear. But Jesus Christ, though risen, was not a physical presence among disciples after about AD30. The founder, in the direct sense, was gone. A whole world opposed the earliest believers. They needed to find order, organization, means of survival.

The New Testament was written in what may be called the second generation, but some of its writings still preserve the sense of immediacy that went with the first. The books at the back of the Bible often seem to be losing some of that immediacy. Whatever Jesus meant when he said he would come again within the lifetime of his hearers did not seem to be coming to pass. Soon people were on the scene who did not know Jesus or his original followers. Later Christians know very little about that moment of transition between the times. Writings from the second century often seem to have missed the point of the Good News. They can be petty and legalistic in character. People then make apology for Christianity through intricate arguments that blend Jewish memory with Greek philosophy. But between the earliest writings and those more remote second-century works appear these closing books of the Bible.

Among them the writings now called the pastoral epistles have an honoured place. Though Thomas Aquinas saw them together serve as 'a pastoral textbook', it has only been for two and a half centuries that 1 and 2 Timothy and Titus have carried the informal name pastoral. The term is personal and implies care and concern. A hint of warmth is associated with the name.

There is a suggestion that the faith is taken up 'case by case', as it were. Whoever writes pastorally has not just come to denounce and prophesy against me but to anticipate my problems, to relate the Good News to me and my circumstances.

The pastoral epistles carry such a personal note. With the exception of the little Letter to Philemon, all the other New Testament letters seem to have been directed to communities or congregations. Not so with these three books. They were sent to a person. Of course, communities are implied. The author wanted to reach congregations through their leaders. The reader today has a sense of eavesdropping or kibitzing, of listening or peeking in on the affairs of early congregational life. But a single person is addressed in each. Again, the reader has a feeling that he or she is looking at a friend's mail with the friend's permission – not hearing a mimeographed set of orders broadcast from headquarters.

Through the centuries Christian readers and commentators have tried to describe the pastorals. More often than not we hear that they make up a Manual of Congregational Life, a Handbook of Church Order. If so, it is hard to picture that the Good News would survive in them. Manuals and handbooks are not designed to impart it. But the pastorals are not so drab as mere handbooks. Only one-tenth of their material includes anything directly about How to Run a Parish – or some other potential best-selling topic for administrators. In one letter, a long section about the role of widows in the young churches might be seen in this light. It tells the recipient more than he might have wanted or needed to know on that subject, and almost distorts the proportions of the whole.

If these were truly manuals and handbooks we would expect systematic advice. These letters pick up and drop ideas, paragraph by paragraph. One can almost never anticipate what is coming next. If there is an order, i seems as random as topics that have first been alphabetized, and then the alphabetical order has become slightly scrambled. Without question a Christian manual would have had to take up questions of administering the sacraments. Later handbooks do. The pastorals do not touch the subject. The reader would expect detailed descriptions of staff positions and duties, but these letters do not care as much about systems as about the persons who lead them. We need the right kind of people, they suggest.

If the manual or handbook description does not satisfy, a second proposal follows. The pastoral epistles help establish early Christian church order and polity. Now it is true that they are regularly scanned and scrutinized for the clues they leave on these subjects. In the twentieth century interested Christians have had to debate order whenever Episcopalians, Presbyterians, Congregationalists, and people of other types of church government try to find means of understanding each other and perhaps of coming together. In such an era it is only natural that the hints left in the Scriptures, which still set the standard for most concerned Christians, be enlarged until they become billboard-sized or broadcast with megaphonic volume.

If these three pastoral letters were all that survived, modern Christians could settle very little. It is true that in these writings church order has advanced far beyond the foxes-have-holes stage of fluidity and motion. The ferment has begun to settle down; everything looks a little bourgeois and conventional. The movement has become an institution. Instead of seeing travelling evangelists and missionaries making one-night stands we recognize fairly clearly defined offices. But from these letters all that can be learned is that each congregation does have an overseer or bishop, a number of elders called presbyters, and some deacons – plus, in one case, widows, who also have detailed roles to play. We also learn that a kind of ritual or routine through which people come into higher positions has emerged. Some sort of ordaining through the laying on of hands is practised.

Once all this is said, however, the author moves at once to the question of the kind of person who fills the office. How should he or she live? How do leaders keep up appearances in the world? Curiously, the author has come to the point better than have many moderns. Church conventions and ecumenical dialogue teams may form impressive committees and study commissions, and do very important work. But the world around them and the people who have to work with the leadership care more about whether someone is a good bishop, an effective elder, a devout deacon, an exemplary widow – not whether he or she is always going by the handbook. So the pastorals may serve to intensify debates about early Christian church order, but they fail us as outlines and guides.

A third way to look at these letters is to see them as a second generation's way of wrestling with and applying the Good News and its embodiments. Here is Christianity for the long pull, the ordinary days, the life of the many and not just for the careers of the heroes or saints. Here is writing that is not likely to ignite faith, but it may help to keep it going in varying circumstances. Now the Christian community is no longer a rather simple family of Galilean and Judean Jews who, if they did not all know each other personally, at least knew the rules of a single game and the customs of a single house. Thanks to missionary activity among non-Jews, many converts have come fresh from paganism. They are being watched People are asking what is different and how they look What is special, what is distinctive about those who are in congregations called by the name of Christ? What today we call pluralism was already there with a vengeance Cities in the Roman Empire were made up of various peoples, of differing racial and ethnic stock. They ha little in common but some vague or vivid experiences of Jesus Christ. They had to have leaders who could help them know each other and know what to be and to do.

Critics often contend that the author of the pastoral letters has not only begun to transmit a tradition but that he has also traduced it. That is, instead of simply transforming it for new circumstances, he has now somehow gone wrong. This question has to be faced if the Good News is not to be turned into Pretty Good News – which is no help at all in the Christian life. In 1 Timothy 1:7–11 the writer seems to have lost something with the passing of the years. In the Letter to the Romans the law of God is seen as an active and vital force that stands as the accuser and even the enemy of the Christian, apart from Christ's victory on the cross and in the resurrection. After all that, it is no longer an accusing tyrant (like Sin, Death, and the Devil). In this passage the law of Moses seems to be confused with generalized law. It seems to exist just to keep the worst kind of villains in some sort of line.

Just as often the complaint is heard that here the real fire behind the first faith has been banked, and only a glow remains. Faith is no longer the situation of being grasped and supported by a reality beyond one's seeing and apart from one's full knowing. It is no longer a gift, a creative act that God undertakes as if to surprise sinners with joy, to give them a ground on which to stand. Where, now, is commitment to Christ or the sense of a dare? In the pastorals, faith has almost come to be seen as one in a string of virtues. Or it implies agreement with a kind of set body of doctrines or dogmas. That approach to faith, carried to its conclusion, has been a problem and not a solution in Christian life. Too often people measure the faith by the degree to which people know and assent to large numbers of doctrines preserved in catechisms or libraries.

So far as ethics is concerned, in Paul's early letters the

Christian life is a total and automatic connection between being and doing. Faith is made active in love. Good works are an inevitable fruit of faith. But in the pastorals the tie between faith and action or behaviour can be seen to be slack or sundered. One almost can exist without the other. Behaviour is a separate topic that needs separate treatment. There seem to have to be a few guidelines or rules as props for Christian living now.

Readers are even told that the reality of God has been perceived somewhat less lustrously in these letters. What has become of the loving Father who approaches humans with the Good News? In his place we find a divine figure who seems majestic but remote, effective but not approachable. Jesus as the 'Saviour' looks more like an idea than a flesh and blood person with whom believers can identify. He is more of a 'mediator' and less of an agent now.

These four observations or charges have to be faced and lived with. There is enough validity to them to keep these books from ever becoming the whole story or the favourite treatment of Christian life. They do represent issues with which theologians and believers who have no technical or scholarly interests have to wrestle. Most certainly people would be less happy and hopeful Christians if they had only the message of the pastorals, with their lack of focus on the cross of Christ, the end of history, the resurrection.

The pastorals' message has to be seen in a larger context, however. Jean-Jacques Rousseau once said that while his thoughts could all be consistent with each other, he could not assert them all at once. In the complex life that Christians live, ideas do not all fall into neat patterns and systems. Yet they can supplement and complement each other. The Spanish philosopher José Ortega y Gasset summarized: 'I am I and my circumstances.' The 'I' of the pastoral letters is in different circumstances than was Paul on the Damascus road at the time of conversion, or Peter when asked to deny or, on another day, to confess.

The pastoral letters, to illustrate, as 'long pull' Christianity, have begun to talk about piety or godliness. This is a term borrowed from the Greeks, and is not part of the vocabulary of the main letters of Paul. A modern commentator, J. N. D. Kelly, speaking in summary for the critics of these letters – just before he responds to the criticisms – says: 'The Pastorals as a whole, it is argued, evince what has been called a bourgeois attitude to Christianity, heavily weighted in favour of practical morality and conventional ethics. The virtues stressed are those of a settled, established community, and we hear much of moderation, self-control, and sober deportment.' True. But rather than be faintly embarrassed by this apparent comedown or compromise, many Christians have found the Good News precisely in the fact that here *their* lives are addressed.

They hear the Christian message and they want to respond. But they cannot all pull up stakes and go to Tanzania on missions. Their moral decisions are not usually on a scale with those of a general sending troops into battle or a physician determining whether or not to perform an abortion. Daily life has ten thousand little trials and temptations.

Today the question of Christian behaviour is again being discussed. Church establishments have fallen or lost power. Old rules and regulations do not always suit circumstances. Pluralism of viewpoint and background is a problem in Christian community. Is faith, in that case, to be only something invisible and gaseous, never touching the life that people can observe? Should there not be some preoccupation with the social behaviour of Christians, the appearance of the believing community? It is not likely that the culture or the circumstances today will permit these letters to be simple blueprints. But they give one a sense of precedent, model, guidance. Someone before our time has had to traverse the ground on which we have to walk afresh.

The case for seeing the pastorals as devoted to *eusebia*, piety and godliness, can be overstressed. Some vigorous, rich, Pauline passages are to be heard here. 'Christ Jesus came into the world to save sinners. I am the worst of them, but it was for this very reason that God was merciful to me, in order that Christ Jesus might show his full patience in dealing with me, the worst of sinners, as an example for all those who would later believe in him and receive eternal life' (1 Timothy 1:15–16). 'He saved us and called us to be his own people, not because of what we have done, but because of his own purpose and grace. He gave us this grace by means of Christ Jesus before the beginning of time, but now it has been revealed to us through the coming of our Saviour, Christ Jesus. He has ended the power of death, and through the Good News has revealed immortal life' (2 Timothy 1:9–10). 'Because I preach the Good News I suffer, and I am even chained like a criminal. But the word of God is not in chains' (2 Timothy 2:9).

No introduction to the pastoral epistles can bypass a nagging question: who wrote them? We have here been talking about second-generation Christianity, but we do not know whether this should mean approximately AD67 or approximately AD105. The ordinary reader of the Bible might ask, 'Why bring that up?' Must all introduction to biblical books give equal time to the scholars and critics who cannot leave well enough alone? These letters say that Paul the apostle wrote them, and has left a personal stamp on many of their lines. Is that not good enough? All the rest represents petty intellectualizing by scholars trying to make names for themselves or critics trying to disturb the faith of simple people, but having to do with issues that do not really touch the Christian life. What would happen to the inspiration of the sacred writings – a topic handled so explicitly in these books – and to the authority of God's Word if it turns out that the question of Paul's authorship becomes unsettled? These questions, though phrased here in slightly surly tones, are naturally and justifiably made by gentle people. They should be addressed.

Yes, why bring up the question of authorship? Do not the letters read the same way whether we see them written by an aged and anxious apostle or by someone else forty years later? In a way, no. Particularly because we are so eager to get the 'feel' of early congregational life, it is important at least to face the issue of when the letters were written. Facing it involves readers in a most fascinating kind of detective work. If they will park their preconceptions at the door for a moment and at least entertain the problem and the question, they are likely to take seriously some 'pro's' and 'con's' of several theories about authorship. None of them can be held without bringing with them some attendant questions or problems. It may be that the issue can never be finally solved.

Yes, again, why bring up the question, since for about eighteen centuries no one did? To be sure, the first person to put a canon of Scriptures together left them out. But his name was Marcion and he was a heretic. These letters oppose heresy and do not present the Good News in the only way he thought was legitimate. It is also true that some second-century fathers who ought to have known them if they were Pauline did not make reference to them. But arguments from silence seldom are convincing. Further, the oldest manuscript or papyrus of the Pauline letters does not include them. Skilful reconstruction – we know how many leaves were bound together in those days – suggests that the torn-off original back pages were not numerous enough to have included the pastorals in the scribe's writing style. But like a child coming too soon to the end of a page, we can still note that he was starting to write smaller and cramp his copy. So there might have been room for their inclusion after all.

In any case, the question of Pauline authorship did not come up until the nineteenth century, when scholars began to notice strange features in them. Here was a touchier case than that of the Letter to the Hebrews, which at least faintly and implicitly suggests Pauline authorship and was long believed to be by Paul, though few schools of thought today think it was. The differences in issues? The pastorals claim Paul's authorship.

The scholars made it easier for themselves and fellow-believers when they learned more of the thought-world of the ancients. At that time the questions of copyrights and plagiarism, of literary property and authors' egos, were not treated as they are today. People then freely took the name of the head of the school of thought of which they were a part and, if they wrote in his spirit, would also identify their production with that of the author. Not a few of us feel a bit uneasy with that suggestion. It will come up again in simpler form with 2 Peter, for example. But there is so much basis for it that fair-minded moderns have to unlearn their habits and relearn ancients' reactions. The letters could have been from some other hand than Paul's, without this fact by itself edging them from the canon, depriving them of authority, or causing the identification to be unethical.

What have been the issues that led so many in the scholarly community to question simple Pauline authorship? The language and style, first of all, differ radically from those of certain Pauline origin. Someone or something – a German scholar or a computer or probably both – counted up the 901 words used in these 3,482 word long letters and noticed that 33% of them, 306 are in no other Pauline book, and 335 are not even in the rest of the New Testament at all. This is a very high figure. A whole new thought-world is here. The author quotes or alludes to Greek writers, as Paul rarely did

Most of all, there are many tell-tale little words, the particles and enclitics – overlookable words like our 'and's' and 'the's' and 'to's' – that give away a writer's style to a computer or skilled analyst. Their arrangement and placement seem to be as personal as a fingerprint and as hard for any of us to get away from as a shadow. The pastorals, most of the way, do not come close to computing out as consistently Pauline in style.

Too much can be made of linguistics and style, and it would be precarious to rest a whole case on it. Winston Churchill, writing a history of the English-speaking peoples or a wartime speech, used a different vocabulary or style than he might in a memo to a subordinate. Thomas Jefferson in *Notes on Virginia*, the Declaration of Independence, or a bill of sale, would leave somewhat different kinds of such 'fingerprints'. Martin Luther King shouting 'I have a dream!' will not always check out consistently with the same Dr King writing constitutions for civil rights organizations. So the fingerprints of style differ, but there can be some explanations.

Theology is the second case. We have already given four illustrations. Where is Paul's cross of Jesus, his sense of the Spirit's empowerment? Why is there now so much attention to heresy? In his other writings he argues against false teaching. Here the author only warns and denounces. In other places Paul really tries to hear his opponents, and loves intellectual combat. Here the writer constantly refers to a heresy, but we do not even learn what it is. It seems to be a blend of Judaism and paganism. Except for the fact that its professors believe that the resurrection has already occurred, we only hear it characterized as full of babblings and old wives' tales and myths and genealogies. This sounds more like a contemporary Communist-baiter baiting a Communism he does not know.

The biggest issue of all is a biographical or historiographical problem. The pastoral letters do not seem to 'fit in' to what we know of Paul's life from his other letters and from the book of Acts. This need not determine the whole case, but it raises questions. The book of Acts leaves him (28:31) heading for his Roman trial. Luke, the author, may simply not have cared to carry the story beyond this point to death or release. It is usually assumed that he went to Rome, was there condemned, imprisoned, executed. In that case there is no time for these pastoral letters. If only Acts had satisfied our curiosity! In order to make room for these letters the sequence must be: (1) an imprisonment; (2) a release and time for new missionary activity of rather ambitious scope; (3) a second imprisonment in which Paul writes while awaiting death 'tomorrow' but still asks that cloaks be sent or that his young friend and successor Timothy should come to him from Ephesus. Even in this sequence, some problems remain.

In the first of these three letters the author is not in prison. He has been in Macedonia. He asks Timothy to stay in Ephesus, where the writer plans to go soon. Paul has been to Crete, according to Titus. He is not making a mere short stop in a storm, as the book of Acts tells us, but is there long enough to help found and nurture congregations. We know nothing about such activities. And in 2 Timothy he is now clearly in prison in Rome, but he has not been there long. His friends have deserted him; can Timothy come?

Those who insist on Paul's authorship, then, have to engage in heroic reconstruction tasks. Donald Guthrie, a scholar who favours Pauline authorship, condenses the critics' view that in this reading, 'history would . . . have repeated itself with a vengeance. Paul again visits Troas with Timothy and Trophemus, again goes to Miletus, is troubled once more by Asiatic Jews, is pursued by the same Alexander, who pursued him even to Rome, and has the same recent prison-companions, Luke, Mark, Timothy, Demas, and Tichicus, the latter on both occasions being sent to Ephesus.' Yet Guthrie judges that 'these data . . . form a precarious basis for claiming a repetition of history.' Paul could have been involved in each twice, and coincidentally.

For such reasons some scholars have thought that the pastoral epistles were written by a follower of Paul who gathered together many authentic fragments of Paul's letters. A forger or impostor would have had to be a genius to think up all the details like that of the cloak, or the counsel to Timothy to take a little wine for his stomach's sake, or the recall that Onesiphorus cheered Paul with his prison visits. These have the ring of authenticity. In this case, there is enough of Paul in the pastorals to make them Pauline, even though the disciple-editor has strung them together in his own way. (A question remains: why should he do it in three letters when one would do?)

The theories about alternatives to Pauline authorship are as full of complication and puzzle as are those that support it. While the large majority in the scholarly community do not see Paul as the author, there are prestigious exceptions. A recent one is J. N. D. Kelly. He agrees that the idea that ancients published in the name of their teachers or heroes is no shocker. But 'it is quite another thing to fabricate for it a detailed framework of concrete personal allusions, reminiscences, and messages, not to mention outbursts of intensely personal feeling, which one knows to be pure fiction but which one puts together with the object of creating an air of verisimilitude.' If scholars can get over the idea that Acts 28 tells the final chapter in the apostle's career, he says, the other questions are addressable if not soluble. No one can be certain.

The letters could have come from the mouth but not the hand of Paul, dictated through a secretary or ama-uensis, as was often the case in the letters that are assuredly his. In the ancient world these secretaries often did a great deal of reconstructing, free adapting, editing, transforming. Picture Paul an aged, anxious, eager, imprisoned man. The Church situation has changed. He has new second-generation issues on his mind and for their agenda. The pastorals could have been born in this situation or in some combination of this situation with the one that sees a later editor working with Pauline fragments. Both can be more satisfying suggestions than the ideas that a wholly unchanged Paul wrote these letters or, on the other hand, that a forger did and they were then worked into the canon.

Those with literary or detective interests may go further on the question. Most readers, having faced the issue squarely, will want to get to the meat of these letters, knowing that whether they issue from AD67 or from early in the second century, they give us angles on the community that heard the Good News, points of view that would otherwise be lost. Thus they address our circumstances in surprisingly helpful ways.

2. THE FIRST LETTER
TO TIMOTHY

Like most proper Greek letters, this one begins with a greeting to Timothy, 'my true son in the faith'. But it also speaks directly to latter-day believers. The author claims authority. He speaks by order of God. God is 'our Saviour' (v. 1), a common phrase in the pastorals but almost unused elsewhere in the New Testament. Readers then and now should not be shocked at the use here of a term that Paul usually applies only to Jesus. The Old Testament regularly speaks of God as a saviour. 1 Timothy appeared at a time when Roman emperors and the gods of mystery religions were often spoken of as saviours. This greeting might very well imply a little sneer at false saviours and a reminder that God rescues people.

Christ Jesus is 'our hope'. This kind of word can be tucked away so subtly and quietly that the reader may miss it by force of habit. Yet it suggests a startling idea: that someone who to the ordinary mind existed in the past, in memory, should actually be a hope for later times ought to be an attention-getting thought. Because Christ is experienced as risen from the dead and present in the congregation, his promise is still ahead of Christians. In a world of discouragement and confusion, he not only represents or reminds people of hope but he continues to offer it.

Warnings against False Teaching

In Ephesus, the hub and centre of much Christian activity in Asia Minor, 'some people' are creating disturbances. Timothy is to put a stop to them. 'Some people': is it charity that prevents the writer from naming them? Is it good strategy to be vague? Probably everyone who would hear from Timothy would know at once who these unnamed 'people' are. Even today it is not necessary to specify who the disrupters of faith are when the heart of the believing community is threatened. Everyone knows.

Instead of debating, the author – who is soon to show that he is not very enthusiastic about argument – simply wants the false teachers to be told to give up their habits. This technique may not always silence or convince people, but in the young congregations the word of pastors and evangelists who could be trusted might have had the effect at least of pulling the waverers into line. Their false teachings include 'legends and long lists of names of ancestors'. Evidently a mixture of Jewish and Greek teaching was at issue. The religions that surrounded young congregations were preoccupied with myths. The mentioned ancestral lists may have resulted from Jewish influences. Some teachers at that time strung out roll calls of patriarchs and their descendants as a means of getting support for their innovations. The false teachings 'only produce arguments'. Christianity is not anti-intellectual or afraid of mental combat, but this author also knew that idle debate could be beside the point when faith is involved.

He has something else in mind, something that remains the best alternative to idle argument: 'the love that comes from a pure heart, a clear conscience, and a genuine faith' (v. 5). Love has to be the core, the glowing centre of the new way of life. The 'pure heart' recalls the Old Testament and Jesus' Beatitudes, both of which to such a heart appeared to be the focus of true life.

In place of these strengths, 'some men' – again, they are unnamed – have lost their way in 'foolish discussions' (v. 6). A little passage on the Law follows, with a number of verses that by no means tell us all that is to be thought of when the Law is mentioned. In Paul's letters the Law is usually an accuser that throws people on the mercy of God. Apart from its role in causing people to learn of sins they had overlooked and to lead them to despair of their virtues, it might also alert people to a care for their neighbours. But here Moses' law, the Ten Commandments, is blended with law in general. Law, the writer says, is made 'not for good people, but for lawbreakers and criminals'. His list of them is rather horrendous, including murderers of fathers and mothers, sexual perverts, and kidnappers. The law is to deter all of them, to cause them to curb their worst impulses. Christians would have a rather limited concept of the divine Law were it restricted to this curbing activity. But while these verses do not give us a full picture, they also do not contradict what Paul has said about the Law in Romans 7:7-25.

In place of the perversions of the Law and of godly living, people are to turn to 'true teaching', which is a characteristic phrase in these letters. This teaching is 'the Good News'. Later readers may not find talk about the power of God when it is reduced to 'true teaching' very attractive, but the writer evidently felt that it had to be mentioned in the face of falsehoods that might lead people to miss the point of the saving message.

Gratitude for God's Mercy

An ensuing personal section, one of the most memorable in the pastoral letters, speaks to the hearts of people who have been turned around in their life by faith in Christ. Those who reject Paul's authorship either have to see this part as a reconstruction of his biography or as a snippet of Pauline material available to and used by a later editor or writer. In either case, it is true to his experiences and authenticates the words of the writer.

The spirit of these words can be applied to both a well-remembered apostle or an unknown Christian today. Christian life is not built on gratitude. Just as people would think it burdensome to find their relations marked only by gratitude ('Thanks for marrying me'; 'I cannot thank you enough for adopting me'), so the believer's life with God is marked more by faith and hope and love than by thanks. But whoever has been changed and given a new outlook cannot forget the agent of that change. Here Christ Jesus the Lord has to be thanked for 'considering me worthy', 'appointing me' and giving 'me strength for my work' (1:12). This thanks is all the more vivid against the background of Paul's past. No one familiar at all with the Bible is likely to forget the story of the persecutor who was completely changed on a road to Damascus, an enemy who became the friend of the Good News. It is interesting to note that because Paul persecuted the Church, the congregation, the community, he saw himself to be guilty for having 'persecuted and insulted him', i.e., Christ. The Church thus embodies Christ.

Believing and knowing are interestingly connected here (v. 13). 'Because I did not believe and so did not know what I was doing,' the writer says, God was merciful. Here is an echo of Jesus' own 'Father forgive them, for they know not what they do.' Whoever has come to faith, has the knowledge that ought to keep him or her from opposing God in Christ. The writer then speaks rather curiously of 'faith and love' as gifts that accompany union with Christ. Elsewhere faith is ordinarily seen as the base or core of life and love as its expression.

'This is a true saying' (v. 15) is a frequent figure of speech in the pastoral letters. The author keeps referring to true sayings and true teaching as if they were codified versions of the Good News. Such expressions do not sound as dynamic as do some earlier ways of speaking. They remind us that the early Christians seemed to need virtual code-words or passwords to condense their beliefs.

When the writer speaks, as he does here, of himself as 'the worst' of sinners, he is not engaging in the kind of grovelling but egocentric activity with which some Christians still enjoy themselves: 'Look at me, folks! No one can match my sins! I'm the worst! Let me tell you about my sins!' Rather than being the worst sinners, they may be simply the worst bores. The author here is instead referring to what he sees as an objective fact. Paul had frontally attacked the struggling young Christian community. He had probably not been the worst sinner in the sense that he had had the biggest pile of petty vices to his credit or debit. Instead, he had opposed the Good News most consistently.

When God showed his full patience to such a persecutor, he provided something of comfort for all his lesser opponents in later ages. It is interesting to note that the writer does not say that he 'was' but that he 'is' the worst of sinners. Not that he was haunted by guilt, unable for a moment to forget his preconverted state. Rather, the fact that 'Christ Jesus came into the world to save sinners' was a daily reality to a man who was both the worst sinner and a fully accredited apostle.

Armed with this experience, the writer can call on Timothy to 'fight the good fight' (v. 18). Military language is not the favourite model for those latter-day Christians who try to be peaceful. But they do serve well to remind everyone of the stakes involved in the struggle between God acting through the Good News in Christ and the immorality or false teaching of people like the unknown Hymenaeus and Alexander (v. 20). They too had been 'handed over to the power of Satan' – was this a kind of excommunication? – so that they would be taught to stop speaking evil of God. This is an extreme form of teaching, not recommended for every circumstance of Christian life. These two people by their example demonstrated that failure to listen to informed conscience can lead to immorality and loss of faith.

Church Worship

The second chapter has led many people to think of this book as the first extant manual of church order. Passages in it do suggest ways to regulate congregational life. In it, from the first, the Christian community is pictured as a praying community. Whatever else occurs when believers come together, they will and should pray. In verse 8 'men everywhere' are asked to pray. Carved figures surviving in early Christian tombs show people lifting up their hands. More important than the posture of prayer is the state of mind. Effective prayer occurs when people in the assembly act 'without anger or argument' (v. 8). The situation of worship life today is no different; when people bicker and are petty, their prayer life will suffer.

The content of prayer draws our attention more than does the command to pray. Jesus in the gospels allows followers to pray for daily bread and to petition on the basis of their deepest and most intimate needs. At the other extreme, he asks them to include his whole saving activity, God's kingdom, in their requests. But here the accent is on civic life and public order. Such prayer seems at first glance to be a public relations gesture. We know that the first Christians were often suspected of disloyalty to the state. In such a case, if they would pray for those in authority, they would be more likely to survive. But a deeper meaning can also be found. Paul Ricoeur has somewhere spoken of Paul's 'wager', his understanding that no matter how people in authority might abuse others, Christians are better off with order than disorder and with the state than without it. Therefore they must see civic existence grounded in God's will and dependent upon his care. Whatever else Scripture has to say about politics, at least it begins by asking believers to recognize the ordering of life to be part of God's plan.

After the appeal for prayer the author inserts a brief

and rich passage that almost certainly reflects an early catechism or portion of liturgy. Its style is formal and condensed. We can picture leaders teaching it so that people could meditate on it or memorize it. Perhaps it was used when people were being prepared for baptism. One of the deepest problems of Christian understanding is locked into it; followers of Christ have never been able to solve its mystery or resolve its difficulty. The Good News says that God wants *all* men to be saved (v. 4). But it also pictures this saving activity occurring through *one* story, one route, one agency. Here the connection between God and man is through *one* who brings together, the man Christ Jesus (v. 5). The term used here implies mediation. It is possible that this formula includes two attacks. The first is against those Greeks who refused to believe in one God or the Gnostics who believed in many intermediaries. The other opposed those Jews who did not accept the man Christ Jesus as the agent of redemption.

After this profound section we come face to face with what many of our contemporaries regard to be one of the least attractive portions of the letter. The author 'puts women down'. The effect of these words can be softened by several reminders. The Jewish and Greek worlds alike placed extreme limits on women's roles. Christianity offered a liberating message. Perhaps some listeners took this liberty too far and began to offend or dominate others. The calls here for sensible dress were in order in the midst of a showy and superficial culture. Adornment 'with good deeds' is always in place among both men and women (vv. 9–10).

The problem for moderns comes when this letter restricts the participation of women in worship and teaching even more severely than did Paul's first Corinthian letter. Here again, keeping the early Christian situation in mind is helpful. But not all readers have been happy with the reasons given for women's submission. Adam and Eve, treated here as historical figures, were also seen as types for all humanity (vv. 13–14). The reference to the Genesis story makes it appear as if woman receives special blame for the human fall. This idea would seem to limit the usual biblical notion of humans' equal responsibility, guilt, and need. And when we further hear that 'a woman will be saved through having children' (v. 15), we need the full dose of the rest of the last verse for balance: 'if she perseveres in faith and love and holiness.'

Unless the earlier words about childbirth are trying to convey some notion lost to us today, they would seem to run counter to Paul's idea of being saved by grace through faith. It is quite likely that nothing more is meant than that women will be saved when they fulfil quiet roles in life, without holding positions of leadership in the Church. Taken by itself the passage is harsh and incomplete. It needs to be associated with Paul's idea that in Christ male/female status differences have been overcome (Galatians 3:28).

Leaders in the Church; Helpers in the Church

If the section on women strikes moderns as being beside the point or even offensive because it seems tied to cultural conditions that they do not any longer share or based on biblical arguments that do not tell the whole story, this next paragraph on church leadership is to the point. Many churches read it as part of the order of worship when someone is being ordained or commissioned to a ministry. Church leaders make up only a small minority of the members anywhere, but their importance is obvious. Badly led congregations, no matter how much lay talent they possess, are handicapped. Much as the Church today wants to minimize clericalism, it is hard to get away from the idea that effective leaders are crucial to congregations.

Those who open this letter for answers to all their

questions about church order are disappointed. The leaders spoken of here are called *episkopoi*, bishops (v. 1). But nothing is said of the duties of bishops. The whole accent falls on their character. Even more surprising is the discovery that what is demanded of them is little different in most respects than what one expects from a political leader. In those days as in our own – one thinks of America after the Watergate scandals – civic rulers could fall under suspicion. It is difficult to get people of high quality to risk exposure to public scrutiny in political life. Early Christians had the same problems, exaggerated by the fact that in the eyes of their communities religious leadership as such did not bring with it the glories that secular life might. Therefore it had become almost proverbial to say that 'if a man is eager to be a church leader he desires an excellent work' (v. 1).

Many of a leader's desired qualities seem to be so obvious that they might almost induce a yawn. Who would expect to put confidence in someone who is full of fault in the eyes of the public, who is not sober or self-controlled or orderly, is unable to teach, drunk or violent, money-grubbing? Two lines *do* stand out. He must 'have only one wife' (v. 2). Since the practice of having many wives, polygamy, was not allowed for any Christians, it would hardly be a temptation for leaders. Four or five different explanations have been suggested. One of the more jarring suggestions, in the eyes of moderns, is probably the appropriate one: he should be or have been married only once. Should there have been a divorce or if he had been widowed, special virtue would be attached to his remaining in an unmarried state thereafter. Whatever all this meant then, today little more is associated with this word than the idea that church leaders should have their marital and familial life in control and that they should be exemplary. From then until now the families of religious leaders have always been under close observation – perhaps *too* close. 1

Timothy does not expect superhuman character from the leaders, and in a subsequent section we see that this writing assumes that 'helpers', deacons and their wives (v. 11) or, some say, deaconesses, should have the same virtues and refrain from the same vices.

The other interesting requirement: leaders should not be recent converts. Some see here a proof that this letter was written several decades after the birth of the Church, since the Church at Ephesus in Paul's lifetime could only have been made up of recent converts. But recency is relative. People who have been part of a movement only two or three years look at new recruits as being immature and unready. Whatever the time scale, the intent is clear. New converts may be too fervent and rootless to have perspective or be trustworthy. Let them be seasoned a bit before they take the most responsible posts.

The Great Secret

The chapter closes with a bridge or hinge section. Certainly it interrupts the idea that this is a simple manual of church order, thumb-indexed and ready to use. What must have been a little Christian hymn suddenly erupts. Those who are disappointed that it does not include hints of the central Christian truth – there is here no cross and no resurrection – might do well to look in today's hymnals. Most Christian songs must limit themselves to a single idea. This six-line stanza concentrates on how Jesus Christ was believed, glorified, and proclaimed in 'the church of the living God, [as] the pillar and support of the truth' – this also sounds like a formula – in 'God's household' (v. 15), a charming and intimate picture of what a congregation is or should be.

False Teachers

The Good News of what God is doing in Christ has always been under challenge. The earliest Church was especially threatened. Just as a young bent tree grows into a large twisted object, the young Church will develop into something distorted if it is bent or broken early. This letter therefore devotes much attention to true and false teaching. The writer is not surprised that attacks on truth or loss of faith are occurring: 'The Spirit says clearly that some men will abandon the faith in later times' (v. 1). No doubt this refers to what numerous early Christian prophets, speaking in the Spirit, had been saying.

False teaching rises from 'lying spirits' and 'the teachings of demons'. The demonic has been defined as a mode of existence that is always in the process of destroying itself and everything with which it comes into contact. The 'demonic' heresies did not prevail. But without strenuous effort they might have destroyed the truth. Here two clues about the false teachings are provided. Those who hold them are opposed to marriage and to eating certain foods. But 'everything that God has created is good', so marriage and food are at least potentially good. They are so actually when they are associated with prayer and the giving of thanks. These make food 'acceptable to God' (v. 5). Here may be a hint of the thanksgiving that went and goes with the Lord's Supper. Or it may have only reminded young congregations of the Old Testament and Judaism's practice of blessing and thanking for food.

Subsequent Christians have always had difficulty learning that God's creation is good, to be enjoyed by those who respond to the Good News. Of course, their lives are to be disciplined and they are not to engage in excess. But the idea that marriage is an inferior state or that there are taboos about what foods may be eaten and at which times runs counter to the concept of the good that comes with thankful understanding.

A Good Servant of Christ Jesus

Support or rejection of truth comes not through disembodied ideas but through living people. If Timothy or any later church leader or helper is to confront evil, he will have to be a plausible servant of Christ Jesus. The writer gives several prescriptions. Feed yourself on words of faith. Avoid futile 'godless legends' (vv. 6–7). Whoever knows the premium put on athletics in the ancient world or looks around at the obsession with sports today will have no difficulty with the idea that physical exercise received much attention and could be used as a model for spiritual exercise. The spiritual version is preferable because it 'promises life both for now and for the future' (v. 8).

A rather warm and pleasant paragraph follows. Often young leaders' gifts and achievements can be disdained by an attack on their age. Timothy should not let anyone despise him because he was young. How can one change the attitudes of people who make such attacks? Whoever sets a good example in every way is hard to repudiate. Timothy should concentrate on the central tasks of reading the Scriptures, preaching and teaching. But he also should not neglect the spiritual gift that is his. Today the Greek word *charisma* for such a gift would hardly seem to need translation (v. 14). The political world and the mass media have adopted it and applied it to people with magnetic personalities and leadership qualities. But here it refers to an endowment that came from the Spirit, though some sort of act in which 'the elders laid their hands on you' (v. 14) also gives a tantalizing glimpse of early church order. The purpose of all the training and all the attempts to be exemplary is to save 'both yourself and those who hear you'. These lines are not a manual of etiquette or a guidebook to success in an organization but are steps towards saving work among others.

Responsibilities towards Believers

The believers referred to are chiefly widows, elders, and

slaves. The section on widows should be troubling to anyone who wanted to use it as a precise guide for church life today. Circumstances differ too much now from those of the context of this letter. But that does not mean that the words are without any interest. They throw light on early Christian problems and prescriptions and reveal an interest in human welfare in the young community. The world in which Christianity grew was not a welfare society. Few vocations were available to older widows. Families were not always in a position to take care of them. They would be virtually abandoned and destitute.

In that setting the early congregations evidently did what they could with those who would otherwise be alone, with 'widows who really are widows' (v. 3). A kind of Order of Widows must have already developed. At the very least, a list or roll of them was kept. They were asked to pray and to perform some minor tasks in the community. Young or old, the pleasure-seeking widow cannot fill this task. If a widow was over sixty – the precision here surprises – and had proved her character, she would be most commendable to the congregation, both for her achievement and because of the way she could be trusted to serve others.

The younger widows seem to be treated more harshly. A modern Christian can hardly avoid the idea, 'What business of the Christian leadership was all this?' But in that ancient world marriages were arranged. People were not very free to organize their whole lives. The movements to which they belonged interfered with or supported their choices. This letter, concerned as it is with the appearances of the believing community, fears both gossip and immorality among widows in the prime of life. Let them remarry even though the once-married state seems to be preferred in general.

The second group is made up of elders. There may have been debates over the question of their remuneration. Not all early Christians or subsequent leaders have taken salaries. Paul himself was pleased to make his living from tentmaking. But by the time of this letter, some leaders were giving their full time to the daily life of the community and could have no other sources of support. Fine: pay them, and pay them doubly if they do well. They need moral as well as financial support. Then as now many unfounded or ill-founded charges could be placed against people in authority. Christians should defend their elders, forcing accusers to make charges in the face of witnesses.

In the midst of these concerns appear two lines (v. 23) that give strong support to those who cherish the idea that Paul himself wrote or stood behind this letter. What later 'school of Paul' would have thought up such an intimate touch as this one, that Timothy should 'not drink water only, but take a little wine to help your digestion'?

Third, slaves. Slavery was so much a part of ancient culture (or of most life down to the eighteenth century, just as it often lives on into the twentieth) that Christians either lacked courage or wisdom to work for emancipation. While the slave status (which was overcome 'in Christ' [Galatians 3:28]) remained a troubling item on the Christian agenda, the major item of unfinished business for those who believed in the freedom Christ brings, early Scriptures only give some attention to slaves' conditions and circumstances. This word is addressed to slaves, not to masters. Many of them must have resented serving fellow-Christians. Not the only or last word on this subject in early Christianity, this paragraph will inspire little positive attention in today's believing community.

False Teaching and True Riches

The final chapter represents a mixed bag of advice, offered without much sense of plot or sequence. Many a letter, and this one is no exception, closes with a collection of odds and ends that clutter the writer's mind. We try to get everything said in a letter, but still need to extend a few parting shots of advice and encouragement. The first concern here is to reinforce the idea that Timothy must teach and preach true things. Here, as so often, the letter disappoints because it neither spells out nor argues against heresy. Instead it suggests that false teachers need to be accounted for psychologically. They are motivated by pride and therefore they are constantly arguing. Their 'minds do not function' (v. 5).

The author's compassionate and moderate side appears in the two sections of this chapter in which the problem of riches is addressed. There is no simple rejection of wealth. That which God created is good is a point too recently made. The rich are not simply denounced. Those who 'think that religion is a way to become rich' (v. 5) receive a come-uppance. Then and now some people look to religion for substance more than for meaning. The Good News is then presented as a formula for success. Jesus' parables are mined for nuggets of wisdom about investments and profits.

In the early community, the false teachers apparently were 'in the religion business' to make money. The writer rebukes them for this and points the faithful to a different dimension of religion. Always the moderate, he preaches contentment with moderate possessions. 'For the love of money is a source of all kinds of evil' (v. 10); the familiar phrase may have been a proverb already in its day. The love of money leads many to wander from the faith.

Personal Instructions

Now follows the shopping list of virtues, the catalogue of good counsels. Here the Christian life is pictured as a contest for which the believer must be well prepared. At the heart of the struggle is his ability to keep on confessing and identifying with Christ Jesus. Mention of the need to remain pure 'until the Day our Lord Jesus Christ will appear' (v. 14) inspires yet another evident quotation of a hymn or formula about God's character. 'He alone is immortal' (v. 16). The Greek notion of natural immortality differs from the Christian idea that ongoing life is the gift of God. The associated concept of the invisibility of God and of his dwelling in light are frequent biblical references.

The book closes with an expression of the concept of truth as a kind of deposit or treasury to be guarded, as if it were capable of being packaged. This idea should be coupled with all the biblical pictures of faith as moving, active, fluid, adventurous. Then the meat of these words can be appreciated: it is easy to have the faith chattered away. Someone must take care of its purity and proclamation, beginning with Timothy and the young Church and continuing into tomorrow.

3. THE SECOND LETTER
TO TIMOTHY

The second letter has more admirers than does the first. If the first epistle sometimes seems impersonal, static, not always full of conflict and drive, its successor in the canon rings with many Pauline accents. The author is himself deeply involved in the issues he presents. His emotions show constantly. While he still speaks of the faith as true teaching or a kind of deposit, a possession to be treasured and guarded and dispensed, in these chapters more expressions of the dynamism of faith appear.

Thanksgiving and Encouragement

A paragraph of winning character (vv. 3–7) presents the writer affirming his past. Christians have seldom known what to do about their antecedent Jewish faith. Only the heretics threw away the Hebrew Scriptures, which came to be called the Old Testament. The believers saw in the Old Testament a record of God's dealing with his people, an expression of his law, a prophecy of Christ's coming. But the major break with the people of that book came quite early – by AD70 the Jewish and Christian communities were drifting far apart. By then converts to Christianity were ordinarily parted from their old home in Jewish piety and worship. Most of the earliest Christians were Jewish, but as Paul and others helped spread the Good News in Asia Minor and Europe, Gentiles came to prevail and there were debates about the validity of Jewish faith. Judaism became the first act in a two-act drama and was not to play a positive part in the second act. In Romans 9–11 Paul corrected that attitude by showing Christians that they were grafted on to the tree of faith rooted in Judaism.

The same Paul was also most emphatic in saying that
the old way was insufficient and incomplete. The coming
of Jesus Christ brought in the new age and the Good News.
People had to face up to the decisive claims he made. In
this context, as in the Letter to the Galatians, Paul could
be vehement against Judaism when it represented life
before God under the Law and not in the light of the
Good News. Here, however, the writer – whether it is
Paul himself or a speaker for the Pauline school and
tradition – reuses other Pauline expressions of warmth
about the inherited faith. 'I give thanks to God, whom I
serve with a clear conscience, as my ancestors did' (v. 3),
is an affirmation of a belief that existed before Christ
came in the flesh.

The next lines are very rich in Pauline expression, and
represent details that may either certify that the letter
came directly from him or indirectly from him through
a secretary, or was a collection of genuine fragments.
The writer certainly sounds like Paul in his expressions
of tears and joy. A reference to Timothy's family tree
seems too precise and revealing to be an invention by
someone who wants to establish his credentials. With
naturalness and ease he refers to Timothy's mother and
grandmother. He remembers 'the kind of faith' (v. 5)
that they had. This could be a recognition of their
Jewish heritage, but more likely it refers to their early
conversions. Eunice, we are told in Acts, was a Jewish
woman married to a Greek. He was probably a pagan who
played no part in this heritage of faith. Married to a
Greek, Eunice would have been cut off from the Jewish
community and the Christian community would now
be her true home.

Much of the opening material has to do with the themes
of shame and courage. In a hostile world, it was not easy
for people to keep their dignity and pride by professing
what sounded like subversive or at least suspicious elements of faith in Jesus Christ. Paul had suffered for his

own confession and, according to verse 8, was a prisoner
now. Prison often shames people and leads acquaintances
outside to shun them. Timothy should not only not avoid
Paul or be ashamed of him, but should take pride in the
identification and prepare himself for suffering for the
Good News.

Here (vv. 9–10) in the context of shame appears
another of those frequent tightly packed passages that
lead most commentators to suspect that a hymn, a
baptismal teaching, or a formula of some sort was being
preserved. What it says is in harmony with the rest of
the letter and with Paul's whole teaching. But now it is
all compressed, giving signs of the condensation that
occurs when a community of teachers and learners or
worshippers make use of some regular phrases. They are
packed with Good News about the strength God gives,
of his saving activity, and the fact that he shapes a
people and that believers are a part of that people.

The whole initiative in his Good News is consistent.
The activity dare not rest upon human achievement
but only upon God's 'own purpose and grace' (v. 9). In a
daring passage the writer reaches into eternity and pictures
that the grace that had been anticipated was now real
in the appearing of our Saviour, Christ Jesus, who makes
it evident 'to us' (v. 10). Words of drama and struggle,
often connected with Christ's victory in the cross and
the resurrection, are here again: For Christ 'has ended
the power of death, and through the Good News
has revealed immortal life' (v. 10).

If Paul is able to keep faithful to this Good News in
the midst of prison's shame, Timothy also can 'hold to
the true words that I taught you' (v. 13). Not everyone
else has done so. A paragraph referring by name to two
deserters and one supporter gives every evidence of being
from the hand of Paul or his secretary. Nothing else is
known of Phygelus and Hermogenes (v. 15) except that
they were Asian deserters. Sorrow over their lapse

is balanced by happiness occasioned by the visits of Onesiphorus. Most students detect a suggestion that Onesiphorus was dead by the time of this writing. It is his family that is to be shown mercy, while the writer hopes that 'the Lord [may] grant him to receive mercy from the Lord on that Day!' (v. 18). Was this an example of praying for the dead? Christians have often debated the point. The words appear here as a simple, natural reflection. What is memorable and can be understood by anyone who has been befriended or visited when in prison, disgraced, or alone, is the example of his having sought Paul out in Rome to cheer him.

A Loyal Soldier of Christ Jesus

In advice to the young follower, the writer seizes on three images of discipline and striving to portray the means of becoming equipped for Christian leadership. The first is again military. Historians of early Christianity tell us that this was a regular picture that lives on in hymns about 'Onward, Christian Soldiers' and 'Soldiers of Christ, Arise'. The pacific elements in Christian witness seem to be contradicted here, but nothing more than a spiritual struggle is implied. No one need insist on comparing all details between the business of killing and the business of saving. Here the point is that a follower should be obsessed with single-mindedness. The soldier who thinks of civilian affairs may be compromised. The athlete, in the second comparison, must concentrate on every aspect of the training rules. And the farmer must be preoccupied with the hard work; then he can have the first share of harvest.

Verse 8 seems out of place, and includes a slightly jarring sequence: 'Remember Jesus Christ, who was raised from death, who was a descendant of David.' But the saying has parallels elsewhere. Perhaps the idea here is to notice the divine character of Christ's activity, which was certified by his having been raised from death

The divine is related to the human lineage. Descendancy from the earthly King David certifies that point, again and again.

This passage introduces once again the image of Paul in chains, suffering for the Good News. 'But the word of God is not in chains' is a remarkable expression of the freedom that no human can take away, though some believe they can yield (v. 9).

Another obvious hymn-like quotation appears in verses 11–13. Reading the lines almost inspires the tapping of a foot or reaching for a guitar. The stanza is rich in parallels and rhythm – and full of Good News. 'If we have died with him' (v. 11) may be a reference to baptism (as in Romans 6) or to normal suffering with Christ. In either case, life results. 'If we continue to endure, we shall also rule with him' (v. 12) looks into the future. The Good News here as so often is contrasted with bad news: denial and unfaithfulness will lead to our abandonment by this living Christ Jesus.

An Approved Worker

The letter can soar and then almost immediately come to earth again. Timothy is to take care to be and remain an approved worker for God. This time the writer is concerned to war against idle and foolish discussions among false teachers. Hymenaeus and Philetus receive direct mention (v. 17). For once, a specific heretical teaching receives notice, but there are almost no accompanying details to satisfy curiosity. The false teachers are saying that our resurrection has already taken place' (v. 18). Some Pauline lines would also promote this idea, not least notably in Romans 6, where the believer coming up from baptism is already resurrected to new life. Something different, probably a Greek heresy, is referred to.

Once again, the writer tells Timothy to stay away from foolish and ignorant arguments. Throughout its history

Christianity has been argumentative. Many of its teachers have used the philosophy of their day to clarify or support their beliefs. Sometimes the result has been futile. But some disputes are *born* idle; so much early heresy was rooted in fanciful talk about legends that the faithful teacher could see from the beginning that he would be mired in confusions or wasting his time to enter the discussion. Gentle correction of opponents would be more advisable; how this might be done without contributing to argument we are not told – reliance on God at this point is the sudden prescription.

The Last Days

The apocalyptic literature of New Testament times was full of expectation that the Last Days were at hand. The gospels record numerous sayings of Jesus about the signs and wonders accompanying their coming. Some of these were to be cataclysms in the world of nature. Others depicted cosmic struggles between forces of good and evil. In this letter the Last Days are to be characterized by the appearance of people with gross personality defects and evil ways of expressing them. The list of these in 2 Timothy 3 is a fairly routine chronicling, almost 'rattled off' as people do today when they talk of the immorality of the times. Most of the adjectives (selfish, greedy, boastful, conceited, insulting, disobedient, ungrateful, irreligious, unkind, merciless, violent, fierce, treacherous, reckless, pride-swollen, vv. 2–3) are expected and are not particularly interesting. One can hardly picture that the readers of the letter were supposed to meditate on each so much as they were to be overwhelmed by the number of problems. In a sense, the medium was the message.

One of the references, however, might point to the situation that evoked this letter. Some 'will hold to the outward form of our religion, but reject its real power' (v. 5). Evidently the young Christian communities were finding in their midst some pure formalists, whose hypocrisy would be evident. A second group is even more specifically identified, for they prey on gullible women whose homes they enter for the sake of getting control over them. They are like Jannes and Jambres (v. 8), two magicians in Pharaoh's court. (Do not look for them in the Old Testament, since they belong to the non-biblical world of legend.) The writer could presume that everyone knew of Jannes' and Jambres' villainies and failure, so they could be used to show how exploiters of the faith in the Last Day would come to nothing.

Last Instructions

Those who suspect that this letter is late, coming from the hand of one influenced by Paul but not from Paul himself, unite in agreeing that verses 10–11 could not have come from Paul, who would only 'boast in the Lord'. The rest of the time he spoke of his failures. Yet here Timothy is to remember nine 'my's' – my faith, patience, love, endurance, persecutions, and sufferings; he should follow my teaching, my conduct, my purpose in life. If this were really Paul writing to Timothy would he go out of his way with such a self-serving list? Advocates of Pauline authorship simply respond that not every time does Paul say, 'I speak as a fool,' when he speaks as a fool. Paul by the end of his life had given so many examples that Timothy surely did not need to be reminded of them. Yet, now and then, writers of letters do speak out of character and toss in some informalities that may not flow out of the deepest philosophy of their lives. The point of it all here is to say that Christians should expect to suffer for faith and that they should find no reason for envying the false teachers, because these will end up deceiving others and being deceived themselves' (v. 13).

Timothy is to stand, instead, on what he had been taught. Even though we know that he came from a home that began with a mixed marriage, now we hear

that even there his Jewish mother took pains to school
him in the Old Testament. Here they are described as
'Holy Scriptures' (v. 15) – the term is unique here in the
New Testament – and they are 'god-breathed' or inspired
(v. 16). That depiction is no surprise. The Greeks believed
that much of their literature had thus been specially
produced, and Jews took it for granted about their
own Scriptures. At this point the theme is not that they
are inspired but that inspired Scriptures are 'profitable'.

In the nineteenth century a British churchman was
being quizzed about the quality of his belief in the then
debated point of biblical inspiration. His formula,
unsatisfying to heresy-hunting dogmatists but faithful
to this passage, said, 'I believe that the Scriptures are
sufficiently inspired for all practical purposes.' Those
practical purposes concern the centre of Christian faith
and the extent of Christian hope. God-inspired Scripture
teaching is for the positive tasks of imparting truth and
giving instructions for right living and the negative
ones of rebuking error and correcting faults. The goal:
that one 'who serves God may be fully qualified and
equipped to do every kind of good work' (v. 17). Those
familiar with Paul's dynamic view of grace and faith
may feel that this is a come-down. It apparently contrasts
unfavourably with the summary near the end of the
Fourth Gospel, where the purpose of New Testament
writings is for people to believe in Jesus Christ and,
believing, that they might have life in his name. But in
his book of practical wisdom a corollary use of Scripture
is not inappropriate. Countless believers still find these
purposes of Scripture to be effective in their lives.

The constant tension between true and false teaching
survives into these last instructions. Timothy is solemnly
charged in the presence of Christ Jesus, the 'judge of all
men', to insist upon the true preached message, 'whether
the time is right or not' (v. 2). This could mean whether
he would get a good reception or not. People will in th

Last Days turn to legends. They will want to listen to people who will satisfy their itching ears. Timothy is asked to be rather aristocratic in the face of all this peddling. The preacher of the Good News will keep control of himself and endure suffering.

The writer introduces a climatic note full of personal authenticity, one that helps stamp this letter or many parts of it as deriving from Paul or his secretary. Here in what would have to be a second imprisonment he looks ahead to imminent death. He awaits 'the crown of righteousness' as the prize of victory for his having lasted in the contest, for having kept the faith. Some of the accent here comes close to letting the Pauline accents on God's initiative, purpose, and grace slip from centrality. Yet it is understandable language coming from a proud old warrior who is now chained and sentenced.

Personal Words

Like many a letter, this one closes with an almost random collection of personal words, recollections, resentments, regrets and greetings. Demas (v. 10), quite likely a Demas who has been referred to in an aside in other writings, is not a false teacher in the sense that he has gone after wrong doctrines. But evidently his love of the here and now, with its pleasures, led him from the Pauline path of suffering. From the inner circle, Luke remains. But now comes a surprise: 'Do your best to come to me soon' (v. 9). How does this square with the just-heard word that Paul is about to die? He has bid deep and fond farewell to a Timothy who is now asked to come to see him. The transit of the letter and of Timothy's response to it would take months. The presence of these words leads critics of Pauline authorship to argue that here are authentic snippets of Paul's writings, embedded in not quite accurate contexts.

Those who favour Pauline authorship feel more confident when they read some tender and intimate touches that would seem too banal for a pseudonymous author to include. Bring my coat (a blanket-like winter wrap with a hole for the wearer's head) and some books and notebooks (v. 13). How we wish we knew what these contained!

We do not know who the Alexander was who had harmed Paul or how it came about that Paul is here described as having stood alone in his trials. But the complaint permits him one last note of confidence in the Lord's power to rescue him (v. 14).

Final Greetings

Significantly, Priscilla, 'Mrs Aquila', is mentioned before her husband; she evidently meant more in the scheme of things (v. 19). Once again Onesiphorus' family is mentioned. This underscores the probability that he had died. A few less well known or unknown people are mentioned and the letter ends with a greeting still heard in the communities that succeed those of early Christians: 'The Lord be with your spirit. God's grace be with you all' (v. 22).

4. THE LETTER TO TITUS

The letter opens with a greeting that is the most packed and confusing of the three that open the pastoral letters. One phrase in it reads literally, 'according to the faith of the elect of God and to the full knowledge of the truth according to piety in hope of eternal life' (vv. 1–2). Not too much need be made of this difficulty: the greeting has a bit of the formal and formulistic character. Readers could unpack it and take it apart because its many phrases reminded them of what they had often heard. The God 'who does not lie' had promised eternal life, and now had revealed it 'at the right time' (v. 3). The apostle was to proclaim the message.

Titus' Work in Crete

Crete: the name here calls to mind difficulties about the authorship and dating of this letter. From Acts we know that Paul's boat touched the island during his first trip to Rome. From Acts and his letters we know of no place to fit in a visit to Crete that would lead to the establishment of churches in every town, yet such churches are mentioned here. But the possibility cannot be ruled out that a longer visit did occur between two Roman imprisonments. The faith was then spreading rapidly and word could have quickly passed to many cities. Now Titus is to do follow-up work, to 'put in order the things that still needed doing' (v. 5). His main task had to do with appointing elders, people who needed qualifications similar to those of leaders and helpers in 2 Timothy.

Not much is known about the Titus to whom this letter is addressed. He is not mentioned in Acts. But from Galatians we can know that a Titus was with Paul at the Council of Jerusalem. There he was Exhibit A for the idea that the uncircumcised could be a Christian.

He was also the middle man sent to the Corinthians when they were wavering (see 2 Corinthians 2, 8, and 12). Titus must have been a diplomat, and could be entrusted with the care of new churches on Crete.

Since the passage on Crete is very insulting, hardly calculated to win over warring factions, it is possible that this letter was to be used to display the Cretan example in controversies in other churches. It is hard to picture Cretans being happy with the description of themselves as 'always liars, wicked beasts, and lazy gluttons' (v. 12). True, Epimenides, a Cretan poet himself, five centuries earlier was credited with this saying, but the apostle adds, 'And what he said is true' (v. 13). They are accused of having imported and nurtured Jewish heresies – which may mean that they were devoted to legalism and did mean that they cherished Jewish legendary literature. People of this type upset the church and family for the sake of making money. They certainly were disruptive of the community shaped by the Good News.

The chapter closes with an observation that has both psychological and theological depth: 'Everything is pure to those who are themselves pure' (v. 15). But the defiled find nothing pure, so even their claim to God is denied by their way of life.

Sound Doctrine

The second chapter of Titus begins with very conventional words about behaviour and rises to an important note in which the special bases of Christian behaviour are located. In the general 'house rules' at the beginning the author addresses different groups not by families but by age or role or status. There is hardly a surprise here. The pagan culture at its best then and the humane culture now would advocate many similar virtues. We all like to see older men 'sober, sensible, and self-controlled' (v. 2) and it is good to see older women living responsib lives. In the Western world today not many would want to see younger women confined to housewifely and obedient roles, but the idea that their conduct should keep them from offending people in the surrounding culture is not startling.

True, all this advice is quite bourgeois. Little of the daring that moved Paul and his colleagues to turn the world upside down or even to preach 'out of season' is evident. But the Christian faith has different messages for different days, and this particular passage is dedicated to helping establish good human relations for the long pull of history. Thus young men are also to be self-controlled. Once again slaves are addressed without a hint of personal freedom in prospect, but one new theme is introduced. If they are 'always good and faithful', they will 'bring credit to the teaching about God our Saviour in all they do' (v. 10).

So far everything is quite routine and is generally applicable to right-thinking people of that day. But more is expected when the Good News comes into play. So the author spells out why people are to give up 'ungodly living and worldly passions, and to live self-controlled, upright, and godly lives in this world' (v. 12). They are living with the end-time in view. Christian life is not just a meaningless serial of events. It is a pilgrimage towards a goal, a march towards a fulfilment. That end is in God's hand.

Good News: 'we wait for the blessed Day we hope for, when the glory of our great God and Saviour Jesus Christ will appear' (v. 13). One word in that line has diverted many from the major theme which holds that the future determines the present in the Christian community. That word is 'God' connected with 'Jesus Christ'. Many translators and interpreters have wrestled with it, not with any interest in taking away from the idea of the divinity of Christ. Instead, they note the rarity of calling Jesus simply 'God' anywhere in the New Testament. John 1 is a clear passage, and Acts 20:28 can be stretched to include the idea.

In point of fact, the apostles were a bit wary of the formula, not because they would in any way limit what they ascribe to Jesus but because it is confusing and eventually biblically wrong simply to identify Jesus with God the Father in every way, and this phrase might lead some people to do so. In the second century the church father Ignatius could speak of 'our God Jesus Christ'. But in the third and fourth centuries Christian leaders held councils and wrote creeds and confessions with an interest in protecting what came to be called the idea of separate 'persons' in the Trinity.

Many who believe fully in Jesus as divine in all honesty prefer another translation, and there are almost equally strong reasons to cite it. Instead of saying 'our great God and Saviour Jesus Christ will appear', it says 'the great God and our Saviour Christ Jesus'. In the Greek there is no 'the' before Saviour. Nowhere else is God described as 'great' and as one who is 'appearing'. All this talk of translations can become very technical and may seem to have little to do with the Good News. But from time to time it is valuable to point out that disagreements over translation are not necessarily born of different theological points of view. What is unmistakable is this: (v. 14) 'He gave himself for us, to rescue us from all wickedness and make us a pure people who belong to him alone and are eager to do good.'

Christian Conduct

The last chapter of the pastoral epistles is remarkable chiefly for a reference to how Christian conduct flows out of the incarnation of God in Christ and for a unique description of the meaning of baptism. We know the names of almost no missioners of early second-century Christianity, yet the faith spread throughout the world This passage may tell us how: Christians conducted themselves in such a way that people wanted to imitate them. Their peaceful, friendly, gentle attitudes would be compelling to all.

The apostle reminds them of their own 'foolish, disobedient, and wrong' past (v. 3). 'We' had been slaves to passions. Christianity came on the scene of an empire whose people were wearying of life given over to meaningless pleasure. They were sated. Some were looking for a pattern of conduct and meaning that would elevate and ennoble them. What made the Christians different? What rescued them from malice, envy, and hate? Suddenly: 'But when the kindness and love of God our Saviour appeared, he saved us' (v. 4). Here is a kind of Christmas message, an epiphany, an announcement of God's appearing. We were saved 'not because of any good works that we ourselves had done, but because of his own mercy', the Good News (v. 5).

A baptismal passage here is unique, because while Paul always connects baptism with the idea of being buried and risen with Christ, here there is washing for 'new birth and new life' (v. 5). The washing by which the Holy Spirit gives us new birth and new life is unmistakably baptism, and it is quite likely that these were words spoken at baptisms. Some have said that the writer was beginning to introduce a magical view of the sacraments, as if they were to work independently of the Word and faith, but there is no reason to read such a departure into these few words. They have some parallels in 1 Peter 1 and John 3. Baptism is here linked with the announcement that a new age had come.

Final Instructions

The final instructions are perfectly routine. The pastoral letters have served us well by giving a picture of Asian Christianity in this period. They help us connect the shocking Good News with the more conventional ways of life – thanks to the purpose and grace of God.

5. THE LETTER FROM JAMES

THE EPISTLE OF JAMES – FOR GOOD NEWS, TURN ELSEWHERE. Some such signpost seems to have been placed at the head of this epistle by scores of commentators through the ages. Symbolic biblical road maps and atlases point to the friendly terrain of the gospels, but then faintly suggest a detour around a few of the writings, including this one. Embarrassed scholars and spiritual guides hint that at best James should be put up with or dealt with as a curiosity – much as one regards the book of Esther as Jewish history or the book of Ecclesiastes as great literature but second-rate Scripture.

Why did you become a Christian? G. K. Chesterton answered that the only sensible response is, 'To get rid of my sins.' If getting rid of sins is the only topic that has to be addressed in the books containing Good News, James is of almost no help at all. He is probably responsible instead for heightening people's sense of sin. 'Come unto me all you that are weary and heavy-laden and I will give you rest.' Words like these of Jesus are stitched on samplers, lettered on plaques, preserved in stained glass, spoken as quiet comfort. They are Good News. But you will find nothing like them in the book of James. Not everyone is either sin-sick or weary. But everyone needs meaning. People can endure any kind of *how* in their living if they have a *why*. Man is a 'stalker of meaning' says Jean-Paul Sartre. But people will find few *why's* stalking in this little book near the back of the Bible.

The book is not news at all; almost everything in it has been anticipated in the Old Testament, in other Jewish moral writing, or in some parts of the New Testament that the reader will already have come across before turning to James, even though they may have been written later. For Good News one listens or looks for an instance of God giving himself, turning towards suffering humans, opening his fatherly heart, sharing himself in Christ. But the looking here is in vain. That God accepts us 'while we were yet sinners' seems a remote or foreign idea. James simply does not bring it up. That we who are accepted while unacceptable are then placed in the fellowship of his Church is perhaps implied but nowhere clearly stated.

We can go further in making the case against this book, especially if it is taken by itself. Suppose that only this early Christian fragment were preserved to us. We would then know that someone by the name of Jesus had existed, because the first two chapters each have a casual, routine, and passing reference to him. We would also learn that the people who were supposed to read these words were expecting 'the Lord' to come again. But we would have not a single saying of Jesus. Not one story about his words and works would pass into our memory. There is here no saving cross, in whose shadow believers find hope. Not a suggestion of a resurrection or new life as a result of it breaks into these pages. Here is no ascended Lord – unless one were to guess that he had to go somewhere if he is to come again. The Holy Spirit receives little if any direct witness. The gifts of grace that come with Baptism and the Lord's Supper are wholly neglected; the only faintly sacramental nuance is in James' reference to the practice of taking healing oils to and praying over the sick. The idea that a church fellowship exists to give us a gracious brother and sister, through whom God as a gracious Other speaks to us, is missing.

Enough. Not every author has to cover the same subject. In the little library or collection that we call the Bible books have to be allowed to supplement and complement each other – and even to argue a bit with each other, as James' writing might seem to do with Paul's. The careful reader can come to cherish James, if he or she already knows Christ. The Church would be poorer without this little manual. In order to see its positive place, its piece in the Christian mosaic, we have to ask where such a writing does fit in.

First, it sustains a hint of the Old Testament or the Hebrew Scriptures in the New Testament. It belongs in the New Testament because it happens after Christ and in the light of his saving activity. Its language is New Testamental; its Greek is as good as any in the New Testament. But many of its concerns remind us of both the writings of the prophets and some of the wisdom literature. This fact disturbs some Christians. The early heretic Marcion, who was the most extreme exponent of the anti-Law position, wanted a New Testament purged of references to anything other than the Good News by itself. He did not comment on James, but we can know what he would have said about it. But is such an attitude truly supportive of the Good News?

In our time Dietrich Bonhoeffer, a German confessor who was executed in the last days of the Nazi regime, concerned himself greatly with the question of the disciplines of Christian life and the character of Christian community. His advice: do not hurry too rapidly past the Old Testament. Christians need the constant reminder that they are grafted on to Judaism and to the experience of God's ancient people: Jesus was a Jew. They need the counsels and piety of the Old Testament. They need the attention to the details of living practical God-pleasing lives. In the Letter of James, which despite its good Greek breathes the spirit of Jewish Christianity, these themes live on. Here the Old Testament is reappropriated, grasped once more, given a second life and a new stamp of approval.

In addition to helping sustain such continuity, the letter is attentive to the behaviour and daily living of Christians. Here it belongs alongside the pastoral epistles and is supportive of motifs that many Christians forget. Whoever is caught up in the fervour of the conversion experience or deeply preoccupied with questions of meaning and interpretation is likely to overlook the ways in which Christian life is also a 'way'. Let the first chapter of Paul's letter to the Colossians dazzle you for a while; let your imagination soar and your head spin. Be elevated and levitated with John's gospel. But then, this book reminds us, remember that there are widows next door. The rich are exploiting the poor. People are backbiting and slandering each other. They need to be called into line.

The believer does not live by theology alone, and James lives by theology hardly at all. His book is a reminder, without being critical of the intellect, that one is not saved simply by its use. Formal theology is almost entirely missing from this book. It includes little digests that refer to the perfect law of liberty, to an implanted word, or to the fact that we were brought forth from the will of God. Given the riches elsewhere in the Bible, however, there is no point in trying to gild these references. Here is a book for people who want their way of life to conform more closely to God's will and way. It is also a book for religious geniuses. Sören Kierkegaard, a great if atypical nineteenth-century Danish Christian, reflected constantly on James. For him it counterbalanced all the easy-going Christianity of cheap grace that was on the point of destroying the faith. The poet W. H. Auden has a corner newsboy saying that he likes to commit sins, God likes to forgive them, the world is admirably arranged. That is not Good News or saving speech. James interferes with its mood.

Third, the letter fits in for its glimpses of life in the earliest Church. These peeks are not as panoramic as they are in the book of Acts and in some of Paul's letters. One school of thought tells us that here we learn that the recipients of the writing knew of Paul's preaching of faith over against works. We know that some of them did pray over the sick and anoint them; that they called their community a 'church' but might worship in a 'synagogue'. They were in need of patience as they waited for the Lord's coming and had to come to terms with their poverty in relation to some fellow-believers who were almost on the verge of being excluded from the congregation because of their riches. They lived by some moral mottoes but they also knew something about grace (James 4:6).

Most of all, the Good News that comes with James is a word of Christian care. James is not a flawless person, the only pastor to whom one would turn. But he is sage and sagacious. One would like a James in each congregation as an example of the just person and as a succinct, not always too judgemental, never boring adviser. A warmth and concern comes through his writing. While the Good News is the *dynamis tou theou*, the power of God 'unto salvation', the law and moral counsel in Scripture can also be a power of God, *never* 'unto salvation', but for the care of the neighbour. Twenty-three parallels exist between sentences in James and in the Sermon on the Mount. If the Sermon on the Mount belongs in the Good News – and how could it ever be displaced from its priority in Matthew and Luke? – then James belongs. Instead of being the Good News *about* Jesus, it has been said, this sounds like the Good News *of* Jesus, as preached by Jesus.

This lively character will not leap out in every line of James; one has to become familiar with the book. It is not very clearly or memorably organized. Martin Luther, not an unbiased witness, for he clearly did not like James, was accurate enough when he said that James 'threw things together in a messy way'. (Yet he was also to Luther 'some good man who obtained some of the words of the apostles' disciples and put them on paper or perhaps someone else made notes on a sermon of his. There-

fore I cannot put his among the chief books, but I will
not ask anyone else not to,' for it 'contains many good
sayings'.) Many good sayings: that seems to be the
character of the book.

Some commentators do find an outline hidden away;
they speak of a riddle, an enigma, a puzzle of James.
Was this a treatise written in the name of Jacob the
patriarch? The first verses speak of Israel's twelve tribes;
a certain kind of moral literature on the pattern of
Genesis 49 existed. Jacob therein addressed his twelve
sons and through them twelve tribes. A virtue or a vice
was connected with each. It is said that James' outline
follows this plot. The first chapter has three of these
counsels; about joy in trial, the good gifts that come from
above, and the need for being doers and not only hearers.
Two follow in the second chapter; the first shows that
there is no partiality between rich and poor and that faith
without works is dead. Chapter three adds a counsel
about the tongue and one about false wisdom; in chapter
four another word about false desires and a counsel
about the future appear. Finally, chapter five takes care
of the last three; judgement is near, and the rich are in
trouble; patience is needed; the prayer of the righteous
will yield effect.

In 1930 two German scholars made the connections
with Israel. The first theme, 'joy', they connect with
Isaac, which means 'laughter'. Patience? What about the
long-barren Rebecca? Jacob wrestled with an angel;
here is a struggle for perfection that echoes Jacob
(1:2–4, 12); with many puns and allusions in mind more
connections can be made. But not many other scholars
are convinced; the enterprise is a bit too arcane, too cute,
too ingenious. Would James not have 'tipped us off' that
he was writing in such code? Does not such a style deny
the patent sincerity and simplicity of the author? Better
to think of Luther's picture of his outline as a kind of
messy throwing together of things.

Even messy throwings-together have to have some character. James' book is called an epistle, but it certainly does not follow the pattern of Paul's. No specific congregation or person is addressed. Nothing in the little book has the character of a letter. If not an epistle it also is not a gospel, nor a report in the form of a history book. James is a kind of moral teaching, after the manner of the preaching in the Hellenic Judaism of that day. It is a book of moral counsel, guidance for Christian pilgrims on their way to a better place, homilies that help them locate themselves and help them behave in ways congruent with the Way. Those who cherish James still do on these grounds. Yet it is succinct and to the point. This is a book that says, in effect, that we have had enough talking about God's way. Now we need walking in it. We can be worded to death; we need some deeds. In that case, the medium and the message fit together very well.

Because of its special character and no doubt for some of the other reasons inferred here, James had a hard time making it into the New Testament. For a book that could have been written as early as AD60 and one that comes with claims of the highest kind of authority, it is more than passing strange that not once was it referred to by a Christian father until Origen mentioned it in the Eastern world in AD170. Western writers do not bother with it until the fourth century.

Origen is not lavish in his reference: 'If faith is called faith, but exists apart from works, such a faith is dead, as we read in the letter which is currently reported to be by James.' Early in the fourth century at Caesarea in Palestine, the first great church historian Eusebius tells us that 'the first of the epistles called Catholic is said to be [James']; but it must be noted that some regard it as spurious; and it is certainly true that very few of the ancient writers mention it.' Not until AD367, when the great orthodox leader Athanasius included it in his list

of books in the canon, was its status secure. The great
Western scholar Jerome followed up with a word that
still kept a shadow over James: 'James, who is called
the brother of the Lord . . . wrote only one epistle, which
is one of the seven catholic epistles, and which, some
people say, was issued by someone else under James'
name.'

The status may have been secure ever after, but that
did not mean all Christians subsequently were glad that
it was part of the New Testament. The sixteenth-century
humanist scholar Erasmus thought it lacked apostolic
majesty. But it is Luther who is most often quoted as a
witness against James as Good News. Almost no subsequent non-Catholic scholar has been able to discuss
the book without reference to Luther's harsh words.
Luther, it must be remembered, was given to extreme
statement. He almost never settled for the middle of the
road or the golden mean. He would make extravagant
statements on either and sometimes on both sides of
debated issues. His whole mature life was an obsession
with Paul's proclamation that man is justified by grace
through faith and not by works. And to him James
seemed flatly to contradict this central Good News.

> In sum: the gospel and the first epistle of St John,
> St Paul's epistles, especially those to the Romans,
> Galatians, and Ephesians; and St Peter's first epistle
> are the books which show Christ to you. They teach
> everything you need to know for your salvation,
> even if you were never to see or hear any other book
> or hear any other teaching. In comparison with these
> the epistle of James is an epistle full of straw ['a right
> strawy epistle'], because it contains nothing evangelical.

That colourful phrasing has blighted appreciation of
James ever since, though it is also liberating, for it
shows that people who absolutely accept the authority
of Scripture feel free to respond in different ways to its

various approaches and not to be bound by traditional regard for authorship and status of books. And Luther did say some kinder words, as well. 'I think highly of the epistle of James, and regard it as valuable although it was rejected in early days. It does not expound human doctrines, but lays much emphasis on God's law. Yet to give my own opinion, without prejudice to that of anyone else, I do not hold it to be of apostolic authorship.' And the verdict: 'He wishes to guard against those who depended on faith without going on to works'; so far so good. 'But he had neither the spirit, nor the thought, nor the eloquence equal to the task . . . I therefore refuse him a place among the writers of the true canon of my Bible; but I would not prevent anyone else placing him or raising him where he likes, for the epistle contains many excellent passages.'

Much too can be made of Luther on this point; nothing dared stand in the way of his theme and his canon, lest the Good News be lost. It was another Lutheran, Kierkegaard, who said that if Luther would see what his heirs made of the Good News he would have had to assert the opposite in Kierkegaard's own day. In which case, presumably, Luther would welcome the witness of James. Luther denied apostolic authorship to this writing; a word should be said about authorship.

The book itself makes no fuss about the author. He disappears after the first line and gives no clues to his autobiography and few clear ones to his whereabouts. But he was a James or he took the name of James. (We have already seen that in the culture in which the biblical writings appeared such was a common practice; there are few good reasons for seeing it appearing here.) The Bible presents a number of candidates. There was a James, the son of Alphaeus (and thus probably a brother of Matthew), 'James the Little', in the inner circle. But there is no reason to attribute this letter to him, and almost no one ever has. Nor is a much better known James, the brother of John and the son of Zebedee, a candidate. He was in the 'inner trio' of Peter, James, and John. But in AD44 he became the first martyred disciple. The date is almost certainly too early to allow for the situation that this letter reflects. So if it is a *known* James, the earliest tradition's candidate is still best: 'the brother of the Lord.'

Catholics and those who have believed in Mary's perpetual virginity have either had to see these brothers as 'cousins' or step-brothers, perhaps earlier children of Joseph. But the gospels are quite natural about saying that Jesus had brothers, and a James is referred to consistently as being one of them. He did not seem to be overly impressed by Jesus before the crucifixion, and the gospels do not see him in the centre of the drama. But the book of Acts has Paul saying that the risen Jesus appeared to James. A startling change then occurred. We know that James was a leader and even *the* leader of the church at Jerusalem. He stayed put, while travelling evangelists deferred to him or reported to him. When Pauline and Jewish factions were at odds in the Council of Jerusalem, this James 'the Just' or 'the Righteous' was a kind of moderator in the debate.

The issues of that Council seem to be reflected in this letter. Some commentators see James 2:14–26 as a head-on attack on Paul and his doctrine. There are even in both Paul and James direct references to passages in Genesis, especially about Abraham, but they are used to opposite effect. But others see James' passages not as informed attacks on Paul but independent positive statements directed to people who lived in a thought-world shaped by the Good News but chipped away at by ideas of cheap grace and lapses into pagan morality.

Several arguments can support the idea of authorship by the Lord's brother. He led the Jerusalem church and reflected Jewish Christianity, as this letter does. Some of the phrases here sound like those of James in Acts

15, the report on the Council of Jerusalem. But there are also problems. His Greek seems too good for a Galilean Jew. He can pun, he can rhyme, he can play with the language – all acts that do not come naturally to one whose native tongue is Aramaic and Hebrew and who could not have been exposed to a good education. Yet this argument is not overwhelming; simple artisans are often elegantly bilingual.

Substance more than style puts some people off. If James is Jesus' brother, why does he not mention it? (Turn that around: if you have status, and everyone knows it, you gain greater authority by *not* having to refer to it.) Why, since the resurrection turned James' life around, does he not bring it up, since he wants to turn other people's lives around? How could the Church situation have developed to this point by the time of this James' death? On this scene are well-entrenched selfish rich Christians; how did their practices come to be proverbially offensive within a quarter-century? (Again, in reply, one can answer that social custom is very strong and Christianity may soon have numbered some rich who fell back into old ways.)

Speculation may never cease about authorship, but it is not intense, since knowledge of it will not greatly colour the interpretation. If the letter is not by James, the rich have more time to have arrived on the scene (by around AD100). But then a new problem comes: why was such a book necessary that late? An early book could have 'coasted' without reference to Messiahship, crucifixion, atonement, resurrection, or Jesus' godhead, and could quite naturally still have pictured Christian synagogue worship. Defenders of late-date writing almost have to discover or invent somewhere a pocket of old-fashioned, uninformed Christians who have been afflicted by cultural lag and have not kept up with two generations of early Christian development. Maybe such a group survived in Syria, a group living by simple and primitive Christian beliefs but needing a reminder of the ethical ideals of the Good News.

When these problems are brought up, more scholars allow for an early date and, possibly, authorship by the authoritative Jerusalem leader, Jesus' brother. Neither school of thought can know for sure. We are then freed to return to the uses of his book. Whoever needs the sense of warm concern for the poor and the sick, and the widowed will welcome it; whoever likes portraits and guidelines for behaviour, not as paths to salvation but as expressions of the whole Christian life, will enjoy it. Whoever needs the counsel of patience or support in the midst of aggravations and trials and sufferings will find in its author a friend. Here are traces of a 'royal law', a love of the neighbour that is a law of liberty – Good News!

A French scholar named Marty in *L'Épître de Jacques* summarizes the case well: the author is a moralist, his mind is directed towards the practical. 'The epistle is a masterpiece of virile and reverent simplicity . . . The Christian tradition upon which it draws, though nourished undoubtedly on the profound truth of the primitive Gospel teaching, has become detached from the framework of the life of Jesus, and condensed into a "wisdom that comes from on high" which stimulates the Parousia [second coming] hope, and which has to show itself in actions, and in a sanctified life worthy in every respect of the honourable name it claims' (translated by E. C. Blackman).

Since Luther was a witness against James, let Calvin have the last word for him. 'Though James seems more sparing in proclaiming the grace of Christ than it behoved an apostle to be, it is not surely required of all to handle the same arguments . . . [The letter] is indeed full of instruction on various subjects, the benefit of which extends to every part of the Christian life; for there are here remarkable passages on patience, prayer to

God, the excellency and fruit of heavenly truth [and] humility.'

Introduction

This letter begins abruptly, as many a Greek letter of its day would, by referring to the author and its recipient. James is a 'servant' of God and of the Lord Jesus Christ. The word means 'slave', and is common in the New Testament. It implies that a person is completely obedient to the will of God and Christ. Of more interest is the reference to the recipients, 'all God's people, scattered over the whole world'. This translation does not bring out the full meaning of the original, which referred to 'the twelve tribes in the Dispersion'.

Three things could be meant. James could be simply taking over the very ancient word for Israel, one that could not have been appropriate for centuries but which had passed into habit. There were no longer 'tribes', but there once had been. His sweep was wide. Second, he may have been referring to the new people of God, the new Israel, whose twelve disciples may have symbolized Israel. Third, as mentioned above, a few commentators think he is modelling his book after manuals addressed by 'Jacob' to symbolic sons and tribes. What is important to notice here is that, unlike other New Testament letters, no specific congregation or direct situation comes to mind. This is a general epistle, a tract, perhaps a digest of a sermon.

Faith and Wisdom

James wastes no time in getting to the point, or to the points, for his various subjects are not always intimately connected. First he connects faith with wisdom. Faith here may not be the characteristic faith that marks other early Christian writings, since it includes no mention of God's activity in Christ. Here it depends upon a prayer relationship to God. The prayers will be uttered most fervently by people who are being persecuted. We are not told of any specific suffering that Christians were then enduring. This is the language of general principle. For that reason it has spoken to the hearts of people in times and places that have little in common with the dramatic era of martyrdoms that we associate with the Roman Empire.

The idea that trials are a test of faith and that one grows stronger from each victory is a familiar biblical notion. But now it is all intensified to the point that endurance should carry the tried one all the way, 'so that you may be perfect and complete, lacking nothing' (v. 4). Here is a parallel to Jesus' word in the Sermon on the Mount, which commends to his disciples his own Father's perfection. Somehow when James speaks of being perfect it does not sound radical. There is a kind of Greek interest in a balanced personality, a Jewish love for wholeness. We do not picture a Pauline 'fool for Christ' in these practical passages.

Good News glimmers through in verse 5, where the God who responds to prayer is described as one who 'gives generously and graciously to all'. Faith is a condition for receipt of the gift. This idea can be associated with New Testament notions of prayer but must not be isolated from or seen in contradiction to the more basic sense that faith itself is a gift. The stories in which Jesus deals with sick petitioners make much of the need for faith among those who pray. Some are congratulated for having held great faith. Those who waver and are undecided have not placed themselves sufficiently in the hands of God to be able to accept or understand his gifts. Here (v. 6) is one of the several occasions when James coins a phrase connoting nature: 'Whoever doubts is like a wave in the sea that is driven and blown about by the wind.' Most references to the sea in the Bible picture it as a hostile force, the home of mysterious agencies that oppose and would overwhelm man. The Jews were not lovers of the sea, not romantic about the beauty of waves. The waves represent human instability.

Poverty and Riches

Several times James will contrast the poor and the rich. The poor are religious, capable of receiving the gifts of God. The rich are selfish, believing themselves to be creators of their own fortune and thus incapable of relying on God. What specific circumstance elicited these comments we cannot even guess, but it is possible that even the earliest Christian communities included some mixtures of rich and poor. Certainly the new poor Christians must have looked with some envy on the surrounding non-believers who paid no attention to God but who knew neither trials nor poverty. They needed a means of interpreting their circumstances, and James provided it.

The first part of this paragraph is easy to grasp: God takes the initiative to lift up and sustain the poor. They should take pride in being thus favoured by him. It is harder to understand the rest of the line, to see why 'the rich brother [must be glad] when God brings him down' (v. 10). It is possible that James pictures the humbling of the rich as the occasion for a change in their ways. From then on they will rely no longer on worldly possessions, but only on God's activity, and thus will have a reason for pride. Here again the writer draws upon comparisons with nature. The sun rises and with blazing heat burns the plant so that the bloom and beauty go. The rich man will thus be destroyed.

Testing and Tempting

Both trials and poverty were tests and, thinks James, temptations. It is possible that some of those who first heard or read him may have known the Lord's Prayer and may have been misconstruing the phrase, 'Lead us not into temptation.' These words could lead people to think that it is God who tempts. And the Old Testament includes several stories in which God plays a sort of tempter role. The most familiar of these had to do with God's asking Abraham to sacrifice his son Isaac. But these are exceptional, not characteristic, acts; James never wants someone to say, 'This temptation comes from God' (v. 13).

The idea that 'God cannot be tempted by evil' (v. 13) ought to be so self-evident that it may sound silly. But the Jews thought easily of God in human terms, so they may now and then have pictured him as being temptable. Without question the non-Christians around them thought of their gods as capable of being tempted. James need only remind them of what they already knew, that a perfect God was above being tempted. Similarly, then, since temptation was foreign to his nature, he would not tempt anyone.

Temptation came not from without but from within. Within each person are resources for their own fall. The early Christians remembered the stories of Adam and Eve in Genesis. The voice of the tempter then came from without. But Adam and Eve were responsible and would not have fallen had they not listened to voices and responded to pulls from within. For James, this had never changed: people still are drawn away and trapped by their own evil desire (v. 14). A domino theory comes into effect. Desire leads to sin which leads to death. Since everyone dies, it is not always remembered that in both Genesis and Romans (ch. 5) physical death is also seen as a consequence of and punishment for sin.

After this brief little psychological analysis of the source and basis of sin James turns to an unconventional picture of God. Once again, the Good News shades into his paragraphs: 'Every good gift and every perfect present comes from heaven; it comes down from God, the Creator of the heavenly lights' (v. 17). Both pagan and contemporary Jewish thought recognized divinities or God as the source of light and of the heavenly lights, the sun, moon, and stars. 'Father of Luminaries' is a phrase that has been preserved from Jewish sources. Everyone who experienced the rising and setting of the sun and the motion of the stars knew that they, his creation, moved and changed. He did not. Therefore he could be depended upon. Since he made humans first among all his creatures, no earthly change, including trials and temptations, need divert humans from depending upon him. 'He himself does not change' (v. 17). Rarely do the Scriptures picture God in these terms. In the Old Testament the anthropomorphic, 'human-formed' images of God find him constantly changing. He 'repents', and changes his mind. He turns and about-faces in dealing with his people. Philosophers and teachers of dogma did not know what to do with these references. If God was perfect, he could not change for the better. If he was capable of changing for the better, he could not be perfect and thus could not be God. Here a human philosophical notion of change countered the dramatic biblical images of a God in process, as it were, who was meeting the needs of his people. Security-minded people, therefore, have seized on James' way of speaking of him and neglect much of the rest of the biblical drama. While we are here touching upon a mystery of thought and language, it can be said that the biblical writers consistently picture that God did *not* change in the sense that his steadfast love endured and his constancy could be counted on.

Hearing and Doing

Religion can be purely formal and outward, not heartfelt, not issuing in action. Westerners have been so shaped by Judaism and Christianity that they often forget that not all religions have ethical or moral interests. This is not to say that they show no interest at all in people being good to others, but they do not focus their religion on the idea. Religion may exist in order to get people out of the sphere of action into contemplation or Nirvana. It may exist to provide meaning and explanation in life. The hours and seasons or the places and objects of life are to be interpreted through myth and symbol and ritual.

Biblical faith may sustain most or all of these interests, but it comes to the point of seeing ethics and moral conduct as integral to the life of faith. The favoured digest of this theme in the Old Testament is in Yahweh's word to and through the prophet Micah: he has shown man what is good, and expects him to do justly, love mercy, and walk humbly with him. Jesus in the gospels is pictured (Matthew 25) as wanting to be found in the people who are in need. Believers will be judged in relation to their attitudes and actions. The Good Samaritan was good because he did what the situation demanded. None of these ideas contradict the concept that God gives righteousness and that God justifies sinners even while they are sinners. The good deeds flow from the freedom of faith. This reality is never clearly stated in James, to the consternation of some Paulinists in later church history. But his view of the life of the good is in many ways compatible with the New Testament letters' understanding. Hearing the word is insufficient; people must also *do* the word.

With that as background, James asks his 'dear brothers' (v. 19) – he is never too rough on them! – to restrain anger, filthy habits, wicked conduct. Here and later he will care greatly about the tongue and about speech. Those who are 'quick to listen, but slow to speak' (v. 19), will more likely fulfil God's righteous purposes for themselves. God plants a word in their hearts; if they accept it, they will be 'saved' (v. 21). Once again, Good News is at least whispered.

Another of James' picturesque comparisons comes

into play here: if you listen to the Word and forget what you have heard by failing to put it into practice, you are like the person who instantly forgets his appearance after a glance at the mirror. In contrast, the one who keeps paying attention to 'the perfect law that sets men free' – the strange phrase seems to be an effort to go beyond the idea that law only accuses, is only a guide – will be blessed by God because he 'puts it into practice' (v. 25).

In the nineteenth century Karl Marx and, later, his heirs, retrieved Aristotle's old notion of *praxis* and made it common in today's usage. Some truth is known through *theoria*, which meant literally a beholding, a contemplation. But more valued is the truth that unfolds in practice, in doing. Those who stress this, claim that it differs from 'pragmatism', which has sometimes been seen as contending that because something is working it is true. No, *praxis* holds that because something is true it will work – but it must be worked out. Action and reflection are bonded, webbed, and wedded. James thinks similarly. The perfect law that sets men free is 'true', but it is true for us when we enact it in our lives.

After another reference to the danger of the uncontrolled tongue, James illustrates the concept of *praxis*, of 'doing' religion and not merely hearing or believing it by recalling the need to 'take care of orphans and widows in their suffering' (v. 27). The ancient world and the early Church were preoccupied with such care. Social security and welfare schemes were as lacking as were life insurance or foster-care agencies. Each person was expected to respond to visible need. Those who could overlook orphans and widows would not express what 'God the Father considers to be pure and genuine religion' (v. 27). Here is a corrective to the idea of cheap grace, the thought that once one was justified he or she could live without concern for others. Finally, the Father wants the truly religious to keep themselves from being corrupted by the world. Here is an important half-truth, or a whole truth about half of what the Bible has to say about the world. The world is the created order, pronounced 'good' by God, the sphere in which his children act. But it is also represented as being under a foreign and hostile power (see 1 John), or as the scene of temptation from pure religion. 'In but not of the world': that biblical formula expresses much of the quality that is integral to Christian faith.

Warning against Prejudice

The second chapter brings us a vignette that contrasts attitudes toward the rich and the poor. So vivid is it that some have thought it must refer to a specific bad experience that the writer must have had. But it may be that he simply had a gift for pithy and colourful expression. Certainly it is hard to picture a Christian congregation today that does not need at least occasional reminders of the kind. The little illustration is set next to one of the two explicit Jamesian references to Jesus Christ, here referred to as 'the Lord of glory' (v. 1). If your life is to be expressive of belief in him, 'you must never treat people in different ways, according to their outward appearance.' James shows a Jewish concern about the formal element in religion and a strong desire to see the inner purity of a person expressed faithfully in the world of appearance.

Instantly we can picture James' rich man wearing a gold ring and fine clothes. He comes into 'your meeting' (v. 2). The Greek word translates 'synagogue'. This need not mean that Christians were still worshipping in synagogues, or that this is a fragment of Jewish pre-Christian literature. The word simply means 'gathering' and could be used almost interchangeably with 'ecclesia', or church. What is interesting is the picture it gives us of rather formal worship. There are inferior and superior seats. People have places. It is almost possible to picture a rather officious corps of church ushers whipping into action upon the entrance of two guests.

James anticipates that his readers will show more respect to the rich man and will neglect and degrade the poor. He knew this either because he knew his own temptation, or had been witness to such a scene. He knew that people have an instinct and they act by reflex when a celebrity, a person of wealth or fame, enters. We like to name-drop, to show that we have been in the company of the famous. Even if their fame and wealth are ill-gotten, people surmise that it is valuable for them to be associated with their possessors. The poor man may be poor because he is honest before God. He better embodies the circumstances of most people among whom Jesus Christ's message was first proclaimed. But the Church never quite caught this message. It has honoured the honoured and lavished its gifts on the wealthy while often failing to notice or help the poor. Into modern times in some cultures there were even 'pew rents' that made possible a system whereby the well-off could afford the prominent seats. In nineteenth-century England, when there were not enough churches in new industrial areas, services were sometimes held at early and odd hours for the poor. Few came. James states that if you make distinctions on these terms, you are 'making judgements based on evil motives' (v. 4).

When he says that God chose the poor people of this world to be rich in faith and to possess the Kingdom, he was very much in line with the Old Testament, with Jesus' preaching, and with Paul's argument in 1 Corinthians that not many wise or strong were called. God had chosen the foolish and the weak of the world to shame them. Maybe readers favoured the rich as a matter of prudence and policy. If I honour them, they may remember me. Forget it, says James: it is the rich, not the poor, who drag you before judges and speak ill of you. Throughout these verses we picture a kind of dialogue between James and an implied audience. This was a familiar mode of expression in that day, and differs in style from the little collection of sayings in the first chapter.

In this dialogue James takes the initiative one more time to put a foundation under his moral counsel. God's own law stands behind the need to 'Love your fellow-man as yourself' (v. 8). That poor man is your fellow-man, but you will not see it if you judge by outward appearances. Going by outward appearances makes you guilty of sin, lawbreakers. James could not be more severe here: the moral law is of a single piece. Tear it anywhere and it is torn. You did not commit adultery? But you did kill – which in the Sermon on the Mount might mean simply that you hated. Then you are a lawbreaker. God will judge; he shows mercy to the merciful. 'But mercy triumphs over judgement' (v. 13). Good News.

Faith and Actions

The most controversial portion of James is 2:14–26, for here he seems to run directly counter to the themes of Paul. Too much can be made of the contrast. One of the best ways to see the differences was expressed by a commentator who said that Paul and James are standing back to back, both of them busy fighting off a foe who misinterprets the Christian faith. Paul had to deal with people who either never had been free from believing that the works of the Law, not faith, brought one into the right relation with God, or who reintroduced the idea that they should have been left behind when people came to Christian faith. James had to deal with people who somehow had the notion that because faith saved, their way of life was a matter of total indifference. No longer should they be concerned with moral action.

Because Paul used Abraham (Romans 4) as an illustration of one being justified by faith and not by works, and because James used the same patriarch to make the case for one's being seen to have faith because of one's works, some have even suggested that James is directly countering Paul. In that case, the leader or an authoritative voice in Jewish Christianity at Jerusalem would here be taking on the major mission to the Gentiles, and the issues of the Council of Jerusalem (Acts 15), where the two parties fought, would remain open.

No such dramatic interpretation is finally necessary. Abraham, the father of faith and of his people, would be an instinctively chosen illustration for anything having to do with the topic of faith. References to him course through Jewish and early Christian literature. It would not be wild coincidence to have two leaders seize on him for making diverse points. It is also easy to imagine that Paul's dramatic interpretation, susceptible as it has been to misinterpretation from the very first, had taken over and had been misapplied by fervent followers. In that case, almost anywhere James' corrective word would be in order. This is not to say that there are no differences between Paul's and James' accents and no problems as a result of these differences. One simply need not be put off entirely by the problems. It is more valuable to take James on his own terms, to see what he is setting out to support.

'What good is it for someone to say, "I have faith," if his actions do not prove it?' (v. 14). The word of Jesus is almost heard in the background as James then points to needy brothers and sisters. They lack clothes and food. So the clothed and fed Christians say, 'God bless you! Keep warm and eat well!' (v. 16) – but do not give them the necessities of life. Is this how the life of God is to be lived among humans? In recent years churches all over the world have been torn by debates about 'saving souls' versus 'social welfare' or 'social action'. The soul-saver have sometimes so stressed the need to hand out tracts preach revival sermons, and hold big rallies that the have come out against efforts by Christians to clothe an feed or change the circumstances of sufferers. They hav no more biblical base for such a distinction than do th pure activists. James is a corrective to both.

It must be said that verse 18 presents problems for interpreters: in the imaginary dialogue, James puts into the mouth of his counterpart the words that state his own position, 'One person has faith, another has actions' (v. 18). The problems probably result from the absence of punctuation in the original Greek. We cannot tell who is speaking: a hypothetical person, or James' friend taking the role of James, or James himself. What is to be part of the phrase the man is pictured as saying? 'One person has faith'? 'One person has faith and another has actions'? And to whom does the sentence refer? Probably they are to be the words of an opponent, an objector, and this objector is saying that some do claim to have the gift of faith and others the capability for good works. One can get so deep into a puzzle like this that there comes a point where one should say, 'Oh, you know what he is after, overall; let's get going on to the point.'

The point is that faith without actions is dead. You make an issue of the fact that you believe? So do demons. They are aware of God and his power. But theirs is not biblical faith. It does not demonstrate that they are able to fulfil the purposes of God. Neither can you if you have faith without actions. Here Abraham is the illustration. When he obeyed by being ready to offer his son Isaac on the altar, 'his faith and his actions worked together; his faith was made perfect through his actions' (v. 22). With that later phrase James seems to back off from directly contradicting Paul, who was just as insistent that people should not continue in sin in order to receive more grace. They were to live holy lives, making faith active in love. God called him 'My friend Abraham' (v. 23). This is a reference not to the Bible but to familiar legendary literature.

James adds another and a strange illustration, that of the prostitute Rahab who helped some Jewish messengers by hiding them and then sending them along on a safe route, away from their enemies. Rahab would not normally be a positive illustration today. One act of vision or foresight on the part of a prostitute would hardly be enough to qualify her for exemplarity as a consistent doer of good works. But somehow this 'extreme case' had caught the imagination not only of Jews but also of Christians. Matthew lists her as an ancestress of Jesus and Hebrews calls her a heroine of faith, so the example is not so eccentric as it seems.

The Tongue

James returns to one of his favourite themes in chapter 3. Whereas earlier he had made only brief reference to 'the tongue', here he offers a kind of 'sermonette', a little homily on its power for evil. He does not here spend any time on the positive aspects of speech: speech as a sign of the human. With it, promises are made. Language engenders love and forms bonds between humans. Words of comfort and assurance are central to the Good News. But something was troubling James about the misuses of the tongue. So he writes an essay on its evils.

Little imagination is needed to see why the tongue could be a threat in the early Christian community. Whoever has attended a vestry meeting, a congregational assembly, a diocesan convention, or a world gathering of church people, soon learns that speech can break relations. Many a priest or minister has been displaced as a result of gossip. Many a bond between people has been broken as a result of back-biting or cursing. Rumour, passed along by word of mouth, destroys reputations or leads to panic. Propaganda deliberately distorts information and manipulates people.

James focuses the problem of speaking on one office in the church; that of teachers. It may be that many aspired to it. Teachers may have been people who trained others in preparation for baptism. In any case, it is hard to picture much teaching then going on without use of speech, so the hazards, he says, grow for those who work in this capacity. Teachers will be judged more harshly and must make extra efforts to control themselves.

Two of James' typical memorable pictures then come to mind. First, he compares the need to control the tongue to what the placing of a bit in the mouth of a horse can do. Second, a small rudder directs a large ship. These two inspire a still more dramatic example of the power of something small like the tongue in something large like the body and its sphere of influence: the fire that leaps up from a spark. In verse 6 the phrase 'the entire course of our existence' has puzzled many students. It may also be translated 'the wheel of life', and was probably a current Greek phrase whose full implications James did not understand or might not have supported.

The essay on the tongue includes further images referring to taming animals, fig-trees that cannot bear olives, a vine that cannot bear figs, salty water that cannot produce fresh water. How, then, can someone whose mouth is filled with and used to cursing also pour forth proper words of thanksgiving? All this may sound fairly obvious, but relates to a rather subtle and psychologically informed point. James is interested in the development of a whole and healthy human being who can be trusted for many kinds of activities.

The Wisdom from Above

The second little homily in this chapter returns to the 'wisdom' theme and again locates its source in that whole and sound person whose gifts 'come down from heaven'. The evil heart has a wisdom that 'belongs to the world, it is unspiritual and demonic' (v. 15). This time his picture is again from nature. Seeds determine much of the destiny of a plant; 'and goodness is the harvest that is produced from the seeds the peacemakers plant in peace' (v. 18). Here is a much more positive section than the one on the tongue, for it seeks the heart that will be 'peaceful, gentle, and friendly . . . full of compassion', producing 'a harvest of good deeds' (v. 17).

Friendship with the World

If these words in chapter 4 are addressed to young Christian communities, one phrase needs explanation: 'You want things, but you cannot have them, so you are ready to kill' (v. 2). It is hard to picture members of the congregations on the point of killing each other. It is possible that here as elsewhere in Scripture, notably in the Sermon on the Mount, the act of murder is simply seen as the logical extension of all murderous impulses, of which hate is one. James deals with the exaggerated version of a problem that afflicts most communities, and shows that it issues from impure people, full of bad motives, who are 'the world's friend' and thus 'God's enemy' (v. 4).

Verse 5 is also of interest since no one can find what Scripture James refers to when he says that Scripture says, 'The spirit that God placed in us is filled with fierce desires.' At best one can say that it is faithful to the spirit of a number of scriptural passages and condenses their themes. But it is also hard to know what the sentence means exactly. The New English Bible makes a valiant attempt: 'Or do you suppose that Scripture has no meaning when it says that the spirit which God implanted in man turns towards envious desires?' Whatever it means, it provides James with a chance to sidle up towards the Good News by affirming that 'the grace that God gives is even stronger' (v. 6). Emphatic about the choice between the world and friendship with God, the need to oppose the devil and the need to draw near to God, James issues a warm invitation for sinners to wash hands, for hypocrites to cleanse hearts, followed by a more severe call for humility.

Warning against Judging a Brother

Some people romanticize life in early Christian circles. If only we could escape the twentieth century and regress to the first or second Christian generation, the pure and pristine Church from which we fell! The snapshots of James' album of church life give little reason for anyone to think so favourably of those days. Soon after he talks about people on the point of killing each other, he describes a rather unlovely scene of mutual condemnation and judgement. Jesus' commands not to judge others are remembered in a similar spirit; 'God is the only lawgiver and judge' (v. 12).

Warning against Boasting

James' little collection of warnings is directed next against people who are so sure of their plans and their schemes that they forget that God controls history. Here as before his bias against enterprising wealthy people shows; evidently they were disruptive of community. 'Today or tomorrow we will travel to a certain city, where we will stay a year, and go into business and make a lot of money' (v. 13). Yet no one knows what life will be like tomorrow; 'You are like a thin fog, which appears for a moment and then disappears' (v. 14). Instead, those sure of themselves should substitute for boasting a different practice. You should say, 'If the Lord is willing, we will live and do this or that' (v. 15). Some people have taken James literally on this point, and in the process have destroyed their literary style and offended their friends with what looks like a show of piety. Old letters are often punctuated with D.V.'s (*Deo volente*, God willing). Some people are so careful to interrupt all references to the future with some phrase such as 'If the Lord is willing . . .' that it acquires a kind of superstitious character, much like the act of touching wood has taken on. What does matter is the attitude of mind, the direction of a whole life. James can tell who it is that boasts of his independence of God and his purposes.

Warning to the Rich

One more time James attacks the rich. So severe are his words here and so wealthy are the attacked that it is hard to picture him addressing a situation in the congregations. In order to understand his style here, we must recall the language of eighth-century prophets like Amos, who with many a rhetorical sweep spoke of people outside the believing community as a warning for tendencies of those within. 'And now, you rich people, listen to me!' he begins (v. 1) but he hardly sounds as if he expects them actually to listen. It is too late for them to make effective changes in their way of life. It is all over for them. They made their decisions. By now their riches have rotted, become moth-eaten, or rusted. How could James not know that gold and silver do not rust? A German commentator, Hans Windisch, introduces a rather touching speculation. James and the people around him may have been so poor that they did not know the specific properties and qualities of precious metals. Be that as it may, he is not here interested in details but in the general situation of the rich.

Patience and Prayer

In contrast, the humble 'brothers' to whom the epistle is directed are to be patient for the Lord's coming. They have not put their trust in corruptible earthly treasures. They must be patient as the farmer is after planting. Verses 7–11 are among the few in James that speak of specifically Christian themes, for his reference to 'the day of the Lord's coming' being near reflects the belief of early Christians and is not quite the same as the Old Testament Jew's belief in a coming 'day of the Lord'. With the Lord's coming imminent, the brothers are to refrain from complaining against each other.

Two Old Testament figures are called as witnesses in the closing lines. First is Job, the example of patience. Job was not particularly patient, but he did endure, and it is really endurance that James has in mind. Later (v. 17) he is going to remind them of Elijah's faith in prayer and the power that issued from that prayer.

In the spirit of Jesus, James also warns against the taking of oaths. Jews had had a horror of the misuse of God's name, and Jesus carried this over and intensified it for his followers. James is more radical than almost any Christians outside the company of Quakers and other extreme literalists. Most people in church history have exempted oaths in court or in the face of law from James' command not to swear at all. 'Above all, my brothers, do not use an oath when you make a promise' (v. 12). A simple 'Yes' or 'No' will suffice. His words are a reminder of the self-defeating character of casual oaths. Whoever must punctuate his speech with 'By God's!' is saying, in effect, 'The rest of the time I may not be telling the truth. Now I am. Don't trust me most of the time, but you can trust me now.'

A much-discussed section on healing appears near the very end of the letter, since it gives a glimpse of an early Christian practice. When someone is sick, 'he should call the church elders.' We are not told much about them; are they a special caste, filling a special office? In any case, they 'will pray for him and rub oil on him in the name of the Lord' (v. 14). The prayer is made in faith. The sick man will then be restored to health and his sins will be forgiven.

Oil is associated with healing, both physical and spiritual, throughout both Old and New Testaments. Largely on the basis of this passage, Roman Catholicism developed the sacrament of Extreme Unction, the use of oils at the time of expected death. Catholic and other Christian movements that would restore spiritual healing have also often returned to the use of oils in association with prayer. Today people are somewhat more ready to reappraise the power of faith in health and healing than they were in earlier phases of scientific development. The early Christians evidently were so wrapped up in the concept of the power of faith and prayer that it would not have occurred to them not to put them to work in the face of illness.

The letter concludes with a thoughtful call for the brothers to call each other back when they wander; the act of turning a sinner back from wrong ways will 'bring about the forgiveness of many sins' (v. 20). This may not be a grand Good News climax, but as often before in the letter it reveals the character of that Good News in the lives of ordinary people. The letter has no final flourishes or greetings, no references to specific congregations or situations. That is why it is often spoken of as 'catholic' or 'general'. It belongs to the whole Church, and supplements some of the more beloved New Testament writings with accents that should not be forgotten in whole or healthy lives and churches.

6. THE FIRST LETTER
FROM PETER

That 1 Peter is a book of Good News is obvious to anyone who spends ten minutes with it. One of the most cherished writings in the New Testament, this letter breathes a spirit of pastoral concern and Christian hope. Its Good News comes through most clearly to people in special circumstances. It is a book for sufferers and especially for those who are being persecuted for the faith. Because of this special character, its message will not reach everyone with the same intensity and flavour.

Thus should a person chance to read it while on a Caribbean or South Sea Islands cruise, its full effect may not be felt. Lolling in the sun, looking back on a sumptuous meal, enjoying a game, looking forward to an evening's entertainment and comfortable sleep – none of these are conducive to one's identifying with the first readers of this letter. Because our century has seen a growth in affluence, physical security, and comfort for millions, it might seem that no one needs this piece of biblical writing any longer.

The twentieth century, however, also presents another face. Most people in the world are still in situations of suffering. Most are hungry, ill-housed, insecure, at the mercy of forces beyond their control. For them, messages of hope, that simply promise that everything will turn out all right thanks to the measures of human progress, will mean little. 1 Peter's hope was not even directed at 'mere' suffering – if any pain or misery can ever be called 'mere'. It was written for people who were at the point of suffering for their faith in Jesus Christ. They were about to undergo 'fiery trials' because of their convictions.

Such an idea might seem to separate our century from the first century even further. Millions of 'free world'

Christians go through life without seeing or thinking about fiery trials for the sake of faith. Their governments benignly protect them in their religious practices. In some cultures, a slightly more moral and at least more harmless people, responsible participants in the customs and habits, receive at least faint approval from the people around them. Going to church simply adds a plus to secure life.

That other face of the century also remains to haunt this picture, to show how partial or illusory it is. Were one to write a *Book of the Dead* for this century, to have some sort of cosmic computer to keep track of the nameless, faceless lines of people who have died for faith, it may well be noted that more have suffered in our time than in the previous Christian centuries put together. The death of one person is a tragedy, the death of a million a statistic, said Joseph Stalin, who was responsible for the death of millions. So the computer or adding-machine cannot do justice to the horror.

The memoirs of Christian leaders who fell in the concentration camps, who died in the slave labour camps, who were silenced by totalitarian regimes, serve better to remind us of the fact that suffering and death for Jesus Christ are realities in our own time. Most of the Christians experienced persecution at the side of non-Christians. They cannot claim a monopoly on suffering. But they have a special problem when harassed or threatened. Where is their God? What has become of the divine source of their life? What shall they make of the promises of the Good News, since everything seems to be going so bad?

On a lesser scale, 'fiery trials' come to people who try to live their faith in the workaday world. Not a few of the committed have suffered stigma and slander, inconvenience and embarrassment, slights and exclusions because their way of life did not conform to the one their boss or associates or friends exacted from them. One need not be an old-fashioned moralist, someone who depicts Christians as severe and blue-nosed rigorists, to imagine the countless occasions in which such hardships occur. Not all Christians would 'go along' with military service in every kind of war, with the production of armaments, with deceptive business practices, with the manipulation or exploitation of other persons for the sake of 'the company's good'. And their conscientious objection was born of their life in Christ.

For all people who on grand scales or in quiet dramas of life have suffered for Christ, 1 Peter is a document that breathes life. In our time a number of Christian thinkers have proclaimed a 'theology of hope'. This theology picks up a sometimes neglected Christian motif. Hope suggests that the Christian theme does not belong only to the past, to a time whose stories are chronicled in the Bible and other ancient documents. This way of thinking asks people to use hope as the prism through which to view all ranges of experience. From its point of view, God is the power of the future. He 'transcends' us by being ahead of us and beyond us in the 'not yet'. He gives us what one admiring non-Christian has called 'an infatuation with the possible'.

This theology of hope has done much to call Christians to participate in creating futures. In effect they see themselves becoming co-responsible with God for the care of the earth, the person, the community. They do not abandon the world to the care only of Marxists and Free Enterprisers, Socialists and Capitalists, Utopians and Planners. But it is possible that such a way of Christian thinking might appeal only to those who can be agents of change in history; upper middle-class, college-bred, young and middle-aged people of health. Has it a word for people on beds of suffering? Does it speak to the lonely, the abandoned, to those who will not be rescued by social security, the company pension, the welfare society, or academic tenure? The first letter from Peter does.

The letter is immediately attractive because the reader can know at once that the author cares about him or her. Here is no strident moralist criticizing every move. If the pastoral epistles or James mingled Good News with manuals on church and personal life, 1 Peter's moral conversation is all seen as an inevitable expression of people who live in extreme circumstances. Their counsellor comes at them not from above but from their side. He is supportive, emphatic, interested in what shall befall them, eager to suffer and triumph with them.

The attraction of 1 Peter's tone is reinforced by its style. The writer knows his Greek. Even in translation it is not hard to see him as a kind of man of letters, well-trained and well-schooled in the language. He can turn a phrase so that it stays in the mind. Rhythm and cadence come naturally in his writing. Literary grace marks its every paragraph. But tone and style can also appear to be externals. If the subject-matter of 1 Peter were trivial, we would pay little attention to it.

The substance of this letter deals with the heart of the Good News. Its content is often called Pauline, and its author gives some indication that he has been impressed by the thought of Paul or at least by the evangelical spirit that shaped Paul. If one needed to put together a little digest or pocketbook of central Christian realities, to assemble a shorthand collection of ideas that are enacted in Christian life, one could hardly find a better place to begin than with this letter.

First and most important of all, says 1 Peter, a new age has begun in the life, death, and rising again of Jesus Christ. History and personal existence have a plot, they have a meaning. Life is not just 'one damn thing after another', and believers are not merely the victims of every force in history – though some days it may appear as if they are. The promises of the Old Testament were not forgotten. The coming of Jesus Christ was their fulfilment – and more is still ahead. We can only with some effort of imagination picture how vital such a message was for scattered little clumps of Christians in tiny congregations of Asia Minor in the latter decades of the first century. It must have looked to them as if everyone but believers had the clue to power or held power; but this letter was persistent: whatever the eye may see, faith knows the reality of the new age.

The new age in Jesus Christ was a fact, but it was not only a fact 'out there', a force that one observed. 1 Peter told its first readers, as it tells us, that they and we are free to be participants in it. 'Repent,' says the writer. Do not let your old way of thinking and being stand in the way of God's onrush. The people called by the name of Christ share in and exemplify his life in the world by their treatment of each other, their ability to forgive and to be accepted.

A strong community sense grows out of these two announcements. The message of hope has to be directed to each individual. Fiery trials, concentration camps, and beds of illness may separate one from the congregation. But just as suffering is borne best in company with Jesus Christ and one's fellows, so hope and joy are known in the community where they can be tested and expressed. This community, says 1 Peter, is born of the new creation that God effects because Christ is risen and is in glory – but also present among his own.

A note that comes through more clearly in Peter than in some other writings is the concentration on baptism. Subsequent Christians have not all always agreed on baptism: when, by what means, and towards what ends should they apply water to new believers? But they have not forgotten what 1 Peter stresses: that here is an act that initiates them into the Christian reality, is part of repenting and turning and enables them to experience and live in the new age.

These theological themes are not stated as cold, dry catechism doctrines. In every case they are announced as

Good News and applied to the life of Christians in a circumstance that those in Asia Minor might have regarded as normal but that is only being relearned in our day. They were then strangers, sojourners, exiles, pilgrims. After Christianity became the official religion in the Roman Empire of East and West and then the religion of habit and custom in most of Europe and the Western hemisphere, it looked settled down and established. Christians often made exiles of non-Christians; they displaced those who would not conform to Christian establishment.

Recent trends have worked against Christian settlements. For the past two centuries secular constitutions of civil states have quietly removed Christians from privileged positions, and most Christians now choose not to have laws passed to enforce conformity to their ways. Declines in church participation have often made Christians look like minorities. Opposition to the faith by political regimes of left and right have further forced Christians into displaced person status. They can begin again to look for ways of believing without the help of the state or custom. Thus when 'the people of God' at the time of the Second Vatican Council (1962–1965) began to look for images of church life appropriate to their day, many of them settled on 'the pilgrim Church', the conditions of exile. They looked for music for the people of God on the march, they encouraged minorities temporarily to exist where someone else 'runs the show'. The first letter from Peter is an ideal document for such searching.

As is the case with most biblical documents, especially those at the end of the New Testament, not as much is known as we might like to know about the circumstances of the original letter. These writings do not come to us as contrivances of a committee of authors who were trying to put together a neat canon or code. If they had, our curiosities might more easily be satisfied than they now are. Would it not be of great value to us if each letter began with the who-what-where-when-why-how's that are so favoured by readers of contemporary journalism? Instead, we have the feeling that we are eavesdropping, reading someone else's mail, getting a kind of over-the-shoulder glimpse of an action that concerns us. We gain a sense of involvement and immediacy even if we do not learn all that we might like to know.

In the instance before us, we would like to know more about the author. The audience is fairly well described. It is a collection of small Christian communities in cities of Asia Minor. While the book is called an epistle or a letter, it might as well be thought of as a kind of pamphlet or tract, prepared for general distribution among them. Perhaps it was originally designed as a baptismal sermon, a kind of warning and encouragement for initiates: do you know what you are going into? Are you aware of what God will do for you?

Except for one or two rather substantial reasons, there would not be much occasion to question the traditional suggestion that the apostle Peter wrote it. We do not know much about his later career, and it is entirely possible that he was in a position to be close enough to the development of Pauline messages and the rise of these young churches and so to have taken responsibility for writing to them. Countless Christians today still do picture this Peter as the author of the letter, and there is not much reason to disturb their peace. But some questions have to be raised.

The first, after having been raised, can be answered to many people's satisfaction. How could Peter, described in the New Testament as an unlettered fisherman from Galilee, be the author of a reasonably sophisticated Greek tract? It is true that many early Christians were at least bilingual. A person of ordinary intelligence could quite possibly have expressed himself in adequate Greek, even if Hebrew or Aramaic were his native tongue. But there is an optimal stage in life wherein one learns to write elegantly, and Peter certainly had passed that before he came into the circumstances where he could pick up such a literary style.

However, in 1 Peter 5:12 we read that this writing comes to readers 'by Silas'. Silas (see Acts 15:32) was a prophet in the early Christian community, a man who had travelled with Paul, a person of some note. It takes little imagination-stretching to picture Peter conversing with him, jotting notes, providing core ideas, and asking Silas to be more than a secretary. Indeed, Silas could give basic shape to themes that Peter truly controlled. The suggestion is plausible; it does no violence to the idea of Petrine authorship or the special character of the Bible.

The other question about an early date and about Peter's authorship – the two go together, since Peter no doubt was dead by AD64 or 67 – is more nagging. Why and how could the author assume that people in Asia Minor were undergoing general and widespread persecution only three decades after the death of Christ? In Jerusalem, yes. We know of the death of Stephen and James within ten years. Paul is harassed on his missionary journeys. Most of all, in the mid-sixties in Rome the first great but localized persecution of Christians came about in the well-known incident involving the fires of Rome and the furies of Nero. But we lack even a hint that this action was a general persecution of the kind that could be perceived as a threat of 'fiery ordeal' in widely dispersed congregations hundreds of miles apart.

The first persecution that meets this larger description, say the people who raise and respond to this question, was the one associated with the name of the emperor Domitian at the end of the century. Christians were often Jews, and Jews were not popular. Christians were also, in a way, ex-Jews, and Jews may have pointed to them, to divert attention from themselves. The followers of Christ engaged in mysterious rites. It was said that they ate their God – an offensive and even cannibalistic idea.

To the historian's eye this second dating seems to make most sense. It is then easier to account for the tone and concern in this letter. But those who favour Peter's authorship remind us that we do not truly know the extent of early sufferings in Asia Minor and throughout the empire. If history is silent about them, let 1 Peter *be* the history that tells us about them. The Peter who here calls himself an 'elder' was not an elder but an apostle. Yet early Christian organization was informal. Why not include eldership among a leader's informal roles and titles? So 1 Peter asks Christians to honour the king. How could Peter do all this with the vicious Nero who was probably going to kill him? It is answered that support of civil order was common among early Christians. Romans 13 was written in similar circumstances.

Those who do not believe that Peter was the author also have some accounting to do. For one thing, the language about the immediate second coming is more appropriate for the earlier generation of the sixties than for the more settled-down Church of the nineties or the beginning of the second century. If this is not Peter, why does the author call himself Peter? We remind ourselves again that in those days someone of the Petrine school could gather fragments of Petrine teaching and, without confusion or immorality, call the sum 'Peter'. But many commentators in this particular instance simply say that through some misunderstanding this fine, authentic bit of early Christian lore came to be associated with Peter's name. The question is not easily settled on historic grounds. Those for whom authorship by Peter is an important part of their view of biblical authority do not have to establish an insuperable case, and those for whom the question is no disturbance to faith or theology cannot serenely state that they have a plausible alternative.

Once one locates the recipients of the letter as Christians who feel dispersed, alone, threatened, in need of help and hope, and the author as a very believable, authoritative, and gifted representative of the Good News, the letter can be read as a direct message to the head and heart, still fresh despite the passage of centuries.

Introduction

Peter's greeting is of interest particularly for the word 'scattered', in verse 1. He is writing to Gentiles, the once despised people who were considered unclean by Peter (in the book of Acts), until God revealed to him that they were part of his plan. Now the author can write to them as 'God's chosen people' in five provinces of Asia Minor. They were 'scattered' as part of a dispersion or *diaspora*. This was the word Jews used to describe the way they were no longer concentrated in Israel. Now it applies also to the ever-growing and spreading Christian community.

This *diaspora* is also 'chosen'. The Old Testament is rich in reference to God's acts of shaping and preserving a people. The accent falls not on the people's choosing him but on the step he took to create and keep them. All this was 'according to the purpose of God the Father' (v. 2). Chosenness is both a dangerous and a comforting idea. It is dangerous because it can lead to a sense of pride and exclusiveness. Chosen people often act as if they are the only people, uniquely fitted to carry out God's purposes in history. Others suffer as a result. Prophets, among them Amos, had to remind the chosen people that God also cared for others. Israel, we hear in the book of Isaiah, was to be a 'light to the nations', and other peoples would come to the light through them.

Chosenness is also a comforting idea because it suggests that even when all does not go well and when a people cannot understand what is happening to them, they are to discern God's purposes for them. He will not abandon them, however remote he may seem. He will work out his purposes through them, however frail they may be. Now the Gentiles are to be thought of as chosen to be 'a holy people by his Spirit'.

Holiness involves them in obedience to Jesus Christ and in the act of being 'cleansed by his blood'. The Old Testament people had sacrificed lambs and other animals as part of their worship. God would be pleased and would accept this sacrifice if their hearts were prepared. Now 'blood' had come to mean the death of Jesus Christ. Curiously, after twenty centuries and many church councils, Christians have never converged on a single official definition of what his atoning act, the centre of the Good News, means and how it is to be interpreted. They spilled ink and blood over definitions of the Trinity or the Incarnation, but they have wisely been contented to let the many different biblical metaphors and images for his achievement coexist. Among them one of the most rich in history and connotation is that which sees him as a sacrificed lamb.

This letter is believed by many scholars to be an edited version of a baptismal sermon and perhaps of a whole baptismal liturgy. Since most baptism occurred at Easter, the Paschal feast, when the picture of Christ the sacrificed lamb was the focus of preaching, it would be only natural that the blood of Christ be mentioned.

A Living Hope

I am going to ask readers to engage in an experiment with this letter. We shall follow those many commentators who see in the unfolding of its chapters a baptismal sermon and liturgy or order of service. This approach will add vividness to a contemporary reading, will make possible an imaginative reconstruction of an early Christian situation, and make application of its Good News to the Christian life all the more direct. Suppose it is not what these scholars see in it. Suppose it is only a sermon

referring to baptism, or a general letter that trades on
people's familiarity with baptismal acts and sermons?
Nothing will have been lost or distorted by this way of
regarding the letter.

If we read it as an order of service, the first verses of
this section sound much like an invocation or a call to
worship today would. Many readers may have had the
experience of attending a partially unfamiliar church
service and hearing some crowded and majestic phrases
that have become very formal and rich, but that need
to be taken apart and mulled over later. Verses 3–5
belong in that category. We can almost picture that the
time is the vigil on the eve of Easter. A shivering band
of Christians has gathered in the company of their teachers
and of the already baptized. They are in very light clothes,
because soon they will enter a kind of cistern, to be
'buried with Christ', as Paul's phrase would have it.
Now all that they have learned in preparation for this
initiating act is being rehearsed in their presence. In
just a few lines they are told who they are and why they
are so important.

Good News: 'Because of his great mercy, he gave us
new life by raising Jesus Christ from the dead' (v. 3).
The new life theme is strong in baptism, which finds
Christians having gone through the experience of death
in identification with Christ's own. Now they are to be
filled with a 'living hope'. Hope has to be a strong motif
for the people here being addressed, for they are not
going to share earthly blessings, imperial honours, or
comfort and good name. They are, instead, to be persecuted.

In the midst of and beyond their sufferings they will
prevail, 'so we look forward' (v. 4). Christian life is
not to be wholly determined by any actual sociological
condition. Sometimes faith prospers most when the
Church is most threatened. At other times the Church is
institutionally strong, but people forget its purpose.

Sometimes it looks triumphant, but is ready to crumble, while again at other times in the midst of tremendous setbacks it gains. The Christian is not asked to be full of optimism, which is a mood based on a positive guess about tomorrow, but rather to be hopeful in Christ. God holds blessings ready for his people who 'through faith are kept safe by God's power' (v. 5). The pastoral epistles and the Letter of James never become this joyfully explicit about the Good News.

Short of the end time, Christian converts have to know that with their baptism they are being initiated into a fellowship of suffering. There will be trials. But they are purposeful; they serve for the occasions of testing. Here we can almost picture the people to be baptized given a last chance to back off. Are you ready for all that this act entails? Do not think of it as the end of your troubles in life. You are taking on new ones. All this points to a future 'Day when Jesus Christ is revealed' (v. 7).

The people who received these words had not known Jesus in the flesh any more than had Paul. Like the post-resurrection story involving Thomas, they were to be blessed for believing what they had not seen. They loved and believed in him without having seen him – and they did all this in a spirit of unutterable joy, 'because you are receiving the purpose of your faith, the salvation of your souls' (v. 9). So succinct and pointed are these phrases that instead of introducing or interpreting them, the commentator is tempted merely to reproduce them.

Now for a backward glance. Those baptized into the Christian community were also acquiring a past, one that every Jew knew and about which the new believers must have been hearing. The drama of Jesus' activity was seen to be a working out or fulfilment of Old Testament prophetic words. It is not likely that a Christian of today who would come across the Old Testament by himself or herself would make all the applications to

Christ's life that early Christians did. These 'fulfilments' have now entered Church tradition, thanks to the New Testament, and it is hard for Christians to read the Old Testament on its own chronological terms. The stories of Adam and Moses, of Abraham and David, are all seen as prefiguring, anticipating, or waiting for their full meaning to be seen in Christ's coming. The prophets searched and investigated, wanting to know when Christ would come and what his coming and his suffering would mean. But these events did not exist for their own sakes, says this letter. Instead the author wrote for the benefit of the very people who now were being received into the Church or who were reading these words. Unnamed people – Paul, Barnabas, John Mark? – were 'messengers of the Good News' (v. 12) who spoke by the Holy Spirit's power. People in that period had a lively sense of an order of angelic messengers or angels. They were often pictured as desiring to peer from their exalted places into the mysteries of the human drama. Even these angels would like to be included in the truths that ordinary men and women were coming to learn and know.

A Call to Holy Living

The translation, 'have your minds ready for action' (v. 13) slightly obscures what could be the next clue that this letter may be a baptismal liturgy. The New English Bible has, 'You must therefore be mentally stripped for action.' The King James translated it, 'So, then, gird up the loins of your mind,' which is more literal. Could this be an allusion to the baptismal robes, as the new believers gathered for the next step in their rite? If not, the phrase still serves to show Christians that their new way of life is demanding, and they must 'keep alert'. Now hope belongs to their activity and is not simply a gift. They must set their hope on a future blessing. Over against the desires that had ruled life, they must be holy as God is holy. Just as in the Sermon on the Mount and in the Letter of James, so here, too, the impossible possibility of using God's perfection as their model is employed.

The Good News of 1 Peter is based in a strong historical sense. Today people often lack an identity. They know too little about their families, their races, their traditions. Mass media flood them with conflicting images. They move frequently. They have to be told the story of who they are and what has happened to their people. So it was with the 'sojourners' of Asia Minor, the *diaspora*. They are reminded of what had been taught them: 'you know what was paid to set you free from the worthless manner of life you received from your ancestors' (v. 18). Instead of valueless and impermanent precious metal, the cost of their freedom was the sacrifice of Christ. Here again the Paschal image of the lamb fits in well. He belonged to the plan of God from before the creation. The author has a gift for connecting cosmic events ('the creation of the world', 'these last days') with the personal: all this was 'for your sake' (v. 20). The Good News is always Good News for someone, for you, for us. Just as God raised Christ, so they are to have new life.

While there is only a small paragraphic break in this translation, between verses 21 and 22 the act of baptism could occur. We picture the baptized regathering to hear more: 'Now that by your obedience to the truth you have purified yourselves . . .' (v. 22), they are to love each other earnestly. In the next verse, 'you have been born again' (v. 23) is almost certainly another baptismal reference and will be familiar to any Bible reader who knows the Fourth Gospel's story of Jesus' conversation with Nicodemus (chapter 3). And baptism occurred with the proclamation of the saving word. When Isaiah 40 is cited (vv. 24–25), the contrast it presents is between the nature which dies after its moment of glory and the word of the Lord that 'remains forever'. The conclusion of the chapter is daring but appropriate: these Old Testament

passages apply to what is going on in their lives. 'This
is the word that the Good News brought to you' (v. 25).

The Living Stone and the Holy Nation

The chapter opens with what may be another allusion to
an element in the baptismal service. 'Rid yourselves . . . of
all evil.' 'Put away, therefore . . .' is an alternative translation (v. 1). At the time of baptism the new converts
would divest themselves of their old apparel and put
on new clothes as symbols of their new life. If not part
of a ceremony, these words at least recall that typical act
and call upon Christians to change their way of life.

'Be like newborn babies, always thirsty for the pure
spiritual milk . . .' (v. 2) strikes many as a strange image.
Why, suddenly, think of the Word of God as milk?
Here, again, what we know of second-century Christian
baptism may throw some light. After baptism, according
to Hippolytus, the baptized were given water, milk,
and then wine to drink. The milk might be mixed with
honey and could represent the fine taste of the Messianic
banquet, the feast of paradise for which they had waited.
These words could accompany the drinking or be a
reminder of its meaning. 'You have tasted the Lord's
kindness' (v. 3), is a reference to a psalm ('O taste and see
that the Lord is good' [34:8]), one that accents the vivid
sense believers had that their God was accessible and
rich in his offerings to people.

Now the attention shifts. In today's sanctuaries there
could be a movement from the baptismal pool or font
to the table or altar. The altar of the ancient world was
made of stone. While early Christian congregations would
probably not have had elaborate settings for worship,
they would at least have had a table for the Lord's
Supper, a piece of furniture that would evoke to almost
any ancient, Jew or former pagan alike, the idea of stones.
In any case, the author seizes on the image of the stone
to expound elements of the Christian life. We picture

a transit of the congregation under the leader's invitation:
'Come . . . Come . . .' (vv. 4, 5). The uses he makes of
the stone are rather complicated and have Old Testament references.

First, the Lord is 'the living stone rejected as worthless
by men, but chosen as valuable by God' (v. 4). In Isaiah
28:14–17 God seems to be spoken of as the reliable stone
that would provide strength and security. This concept
was carried over to God's people as being a stone. Zion
was a mount. In Psalm 118 we hear of a stone which
the builders rejected, referring to Israel. Christians
connected Jesus, the despised and rejected one, with this.
He is 'the living stone'. Now the believers are also
living stones for 'the spiritual temple'. In the time of
Jesus, we know from the Dead Sea Scrolls, ideas were
current that a new spiritual temple had to succeed the
profaned physical one since the temple had been ruined
by desecrators. The New Testament several times refers
to individuals or to the community as a kind of spiritual
temple.

Temples have priests, and these believers 'will serve
as holy priests' (v. 5). Priests represent the people before
God and bring sacrifices to him. In the new age the
Christians themselves will be the priests – a shocking
idea in their world, but one with which believers have
lived so long that now they may take it for granted.

The ensuing words to the congregation are among the
high points of the epistle and of early Christian literature. 'You are the chosen race, the King's priests, the
holy nation, God's own people, chosen to proclaim the
wonderful acts of God . . .' (v. 9). A new group of people
has been formed by baptism. They take on new conditions.
They need a sense of morale and self-worth. Christians
were taught to humble themselves every day in every way.
It would have been easy for them to get an idea that has
often blighted the Church in other ages, the notion that
the community should be filled with self-hate and should

try to find ways to speak negatively of itself because of its failures. But psychologists and historians alike can show that people who lack a sense of worth or integrity are of no use to others and might even be dangerous.

The author is here doing, then, what most leaders of people in our time must also do. For example, in the United States in the 1960s the black community, long forced or taught to think of itself in negative terms, suddenly produced leaders who reversed all the images. 'Black is beautiful' became a rallying cry for people who learned to take pride in a heritage. 'Indian Power!' was a cry of the American Indian community. Internationally, a concurrent renewed movement of Women's Liberation prospered with slogans such as 'Sisterhood is Powerful!' Its leaders called for a rewriting of history to help women discover the long-suppressed part they had played, and a raising of consciousness about the understanding of women. These are prominent examples of what has been going on in nations, regions, ethnic groups, and religious denominations.

All of them can be exaggerated and even absolutized into something dangerous. The result would be what might be called a 'tribal solipsism', that is, a belief that one's own group's insights are unique to them and cannot be shared with anyone. Exclusivism can result. People can cut themselves off from the human family. Christians can distance themselves from other Christians. But the employment of positive images need not produce such results. It can serve simply to help provide people with an identity, with explanations and understandings, with motives for service – and in the first letter from Peter they are designed to do all of these.

Observe a leader of a movement or a people in action. He (or she) will describe the plight of the group. Either oppressors have done something wrong to them or the people have harmed themselves or, more likely, a combination of both has occurred. Then their own history is reviewed: you are a people of promise. More could happen to you than has been happening. Symbols of a better future have to be projected. The leader next shows them what action to take to walk into that future. Today Christianity often looks so tired and settled as an establishment that people forget that it once had to be shaped and gathered as other movements do.

So Peter speaks of the plight of their darkness; they had not been a people. God called them into his marvellous light. They had not known mercy, but now they have received his mercy. They were given the promise that they could 'proclaim the wonderful acts of God'. Few baptismal sermons or rallying cries have achieved as much as this one. It is still quoted regularly when Christians have reason to celebrate – or have a need to.

Slaves of God

Now follow four sets of counsel or advice, to citizens, to slaves, to wives, and to husbands. It is quite possible that someone baptizing Christians then or speaking and writing to newly baptized ones would have had all four types in his congregation. The presentation of little codes of living was a common feature in group life and teaching in that day. Certainly the Christians, who were cut off from their old ties, would be most in need of some advice as to how they were to act in the new order.

First the writer gives a motive for these codes and good conduct. Behaviour must be so exemplary that the heathen 'when they accuse you of being evildoers . . . will have to recognize your good deeds.' Then they will 'praise God on the Day of his coming' (v. 12). Peter does not say 'if' you are accused but 'when'. It was certain that they would be attacked. This whole tract is prepared for people who will certainly face suffering and persecution. To outsiders they looked like a Jewish cult, were accused of cannibalism in their sacramental life, engaged in mysterious and therefore probably threatening rites, and seemed subversive of public order. But, says the author, accusations of all these types will be hollow if others see Christians acting well. There seems to be an almost naïve faith that non-Christians will relent and change their way in the face of conscientious witness.

The first code is for citizens, which most of the people would be. They are to submit to every human authority – the emperor, governors, and the like. These have been sent to punish evildoers and praise those who do good. This is hardly an accurate description of any known emperor late in the first century. But this letter shares with other New Testament writings an interest in order over against disorder, and its author cannot conceive of a principle of earthly order or government that is not somehow grounded in the purposes of God. So the subversive-looking Christians are almost to overcompensate and make a point of their dutiful respect to authority. That this is not the only biblical word appropriate in civic life is clear from several calls to obey God rather than men and from Revelation 13, which *does* sound like a subversive document. These words are spoken to a special situation, but they represent what might be called a normal response of Christians to earthly government, as most early leaders pictured it.

The Example of Christ's Suffering

The rather pleasant naïveté about the effect of co-operation and non-violent witness continues in the second code, addressed to servants or, better, slaves. To those who ask why this subject should come up in a baptismal sermon or a letter to young Asian congregations, the answer is simple. It is possible and even probable that a majority of those who heard or read it were themselves slaves. The Roman Empire had tens of millions of slaves, and Christians attracted the slave and servant classes. In effect, the writer tells them that they have enough troubles just becoming and being Christians. They should not add to these by becoming disobedient slaves. In fact, if they show respect even to harsh masters they will be blessed by God. Here he does not offer much hope that their doing right will convert their harsh masters into gentle ones, but they will have other rewards from God himself.

Much as we might be disappointed that early Christians did not call for or try to effect emancipation from slavery, which was simply accepted in their world, we can at least see the rise of a dignity and an attempt to improve relations within the master-slave order. This effort was to bear fruit, far too many centuries later, in Christian and humanitarian achievements for abolition of slavery in many cultures. For now they must settle for small gains in a troubling order of life.

The writer lifts the sufferings of slaves to the highest levels of meaning by comparing them to Christ's own, for he 'left you an example' (v. 21). Peter stresses Christ's unwillingness to lie or to sin, his refusal to answer curses with curses, or sufferings with threats. He placed his hopes in God as did they. Now, beginning on the humble base of a slave code, the author rises to another climax of Good News, one which recalls passages in Isaiah and reflects the incidents of his sufferings about which we know in the Good News stories. 'Christ himself carried our sins in his body to the cross, so that we might die to sin and live for righteousness. By his wounds you have been healed' (v. 24).

Two pictures of Christ close this section and they easily remain in the mind. He is a shepherd. Again and again we read that the picture of a shepherd will be lost on modern urbanites. It is hard to recall what this reference must have meant in the agrarian world, where audiences would know all about sheep. Maybe. But the first Christians in Asia Minor seem to have been urbanites. They were addressed in cities. It is not a fantastic idea to picture that few more of them were shepherds

or knew shepherds personally than do residents of London
or Tokyo today. Yet they could be told enough to find
the shepherd relationship attractive. In contemporary
cities counsellors of the dying still report that the
twenty-third Psalm, 'The Lord is My Shepherd', remains
a favourite; that the Good Shepherd stories from the
Fourth Gospel have great appeal. Maybe some primitive
yearning for a simpler order and a tinge of sentimentality
may be evident in some of the expressions. There can
also be a primal search for kind and thoughtful leadership
of the kind the risen Christ was announced as having
given them.

Christ is also the keeper (the Greek says overseer,
guardian, or 'bishop') of their souls. It is possible that
this phrase reflects primitive church order, wherein
congregations were beginning to have such overseers.
But it also repeats something of the concept of the shepherd as a caring one.

Wives and Husbands

The third code is for wives and the fourth for husbands.
Taken together, while they are still read as part of some
traditional wedding services, they do not comprise a
complete approach to Christian marriage. In fact, they
are addressed more to what today are called mixed
marriage situations than to ordinary Christian marriage.
For that reason more than five times as much space has
to be devoted to wives. Not that they needed more
instruction in general. The problem had to do with
ancient custom. If a husband changed religion, the wife
had no choice but to go along. But women did not change
religion on their own. Now the Christians came along
and began to win wives without their husbands. This was
itself the seed of a social revolution, and documents such
as these had to give very careful advice.

Rather than be disappointed over the issue of how far
short this counsel falls of modern concepts of Christian

womanhood and women's rights – and it does fall short, bound to its cultural situation as it is – the reader might take the text on its own terms as it calls upon the Old Testament and particularly the story of Sarah for warrant. The choice of Sarah is accidentally tinged with irony, for the Genesis stories do not find her notably mousy or submissive. She is a full personality on her own terms. But she did consent to bear children with Abraham, her 'master' (v. 6), and thus was a model for later women.

The writer propagates an interesting concept to one section of his gathering. It is possible that some husbands will be won without a word if wives' conduct is winning. Today there are still debates in the Church about 'non-verbal' witness. Should Christians ever make use of mass media communication or express themselves through the arts without at some point erupting into explicit verbal proclamation of the Good News? This letter does not settle the issue, but it shows one leader at least who sees value in wordless good conduct. The ancient world was as obsessed with appearances as is today's. Husbands will be won by the beauty of 'your true inner self, the ageless beauty of a gentle and quiet spirit' (v. 4).

The word to husbands is brief. Today again we might find the concept of the woman as the weaker sex to be jarring and not even demonstrably true in many physical senses. But this counsel is given in the context of a culture where such sex differences were taken for granted, and is designed to improve relations within that setting. The passage comes to a climax in a beautiful phrase: 'You must treat them with respect, because they also will receive, together with you, God's gift of life' (v. 7). *That* would be a good husbandly half of a wedding text!

Suffering for Doing Right

After addressing portions of a congregation, a preacher usually turns back to the whole group for summary.

So does this preacher or letter-writter. He asks them to have 'the same thoughts and the same feelings' (v. 8), a call for unity that is still being responded to in modern movements of church unity. He asks for concord and sympathy within the congregation. But soon he is back to concern for the relation of believers to outsiders, where again he anticipates persecution and suffering. After a quotation on moral conduct from the Psalms he asks, who will harm those who are eager to do what is good? This is strange language for people in the era of Stephen and James, Peter and Paul, sufferers and martyrs. So he backs off and remembers that the innocent may suffer and must expect their happiness because they are right before God. 'Do not be afraid of men' (v. 14).

The modern reader can picture lively conversations or encounters that must have occurred in hundreds of instances for members of these congregations in the verses that follow 15. Believers were being challenged because of their faith. The counsel remains appropriate for Christians today: 'Be ready at all times to answer anyone who asks you to explain the hope you have in you. But do it with gentleness and respect' (vv. 15–16). Somehow the new converts will suffer; it is better to suffer for doing good than for doing evil. Verse 18 is another explicit announcement of Good News, one that pictures the Old Testament sacrifices, and the representativeness of the priest who also removes barriers between God and people: 'For Christ himself died for you; once and for all he died for sins, a good man for bad men, in order to lead you to God.'

Suddenly the letter digresses and in the next half-dozen lines it presents some of the most puzzling and controversial lines in the whole Bible. Christ 'was put to death physically, but made alive spiritually, and in his spiritual existence he went and preached to the imprisoned spirits' (vv. 18–19). Technical commentaries have to wrestle with the meaning of each word here. They in evitably introduce readers to writings largely forgotten by later Christians: books of Jubilees or of Enoch. Largely on the basis of this line the most difficult phrase entered the Apostles' Creed: 'he descended into hell.' The passage does not speak of a descent or a location in hell. Grant the existence of a spiritual order of being, and time and space mean little. It is almost fruitless to speculate about the where's and when's that the author may have had in mind here. The two bases are that Christ as spirit preached to imprisoned spirits, and that he preached.

From that obscure point the writer wanders even further, and identifies these spirits as having suffered their fate for having not obeyed God at the time of Noah and the flood. The text is interesting here because once again it leads the author to speak of baptism, and to do so in terms that suggest the origins of this letter lie in baptismal rites and sermons. He points out that eight people were saved by the water; the world of early Christianity was full of interest in numbers and Christians continued this interest. Eight had many meanings, some of them connected with baptism on Sunday, the 'eighth day', recalling Christ's resurrection. The people 'were saved by the water' (v. 20). Actually, they had been saved by the ark above water, while others were being destroyed by water. So the author suddenly shifts the imagery and says this water 'was a figure pointing to baptism, which now saves you'. One should not press all the details too far. The letter simply wants to tie an Old Testament story of rescue and a new world with the New Testament event of rescue by baptism and the birth of a new person, a new creation. The promise of God is the key. The connection of baptism and the resurrection could not have been made more explicit than it is here (v. 21). Such words would be understood by a gathering of new initiates on the night before Easter, as it passes towards morning and they, through baptism, pass to new life.

Changed Lives

The main theme of this letter has to do with finding
meaning in suffering. For the baptized, 'from now on,
then, you must live the rest of your earthly lives controlled
by God's will, not by human desires' (v. 2). This then
inspires a comment on the life they are leaving behind.
In their world they had not known mere immorality,
but an immorality that grew out of and was connected
with their religions. Sometimes people today act as if
anything religious is preferable to anything secular.
The ancients among the Christians would not have
agreed: religion then often sanctioned debauchery and
orgies.

The preacher or writer anticipates that the new way
of the converted will bewilder their former associates.
When they express their confusion, Christians will have
a good opportunity to testify about their new way.
Their witness will include a warning, for 'they will give
an account . . . to God, who is ready to judge the living
and the dead' (v. 5). Those who have died, according
to the New Testament, were also to face a judgement.
They had had their opportunity, for the Good News had
been preached to them. One reference in this paragraph
brings difficulties. In the first verse we read that 'whoever
suffers physically is no longer involved with sin.' The
full meaning is not clear, but this evidently referred to
baptism, a suffering with Christ, and the new life of
identification with him. It cannot mean that the baptized
and converted would never sin again; the rest of the letter
shows how vividly aware the author was of that fact.

Good Managers of God's Gifts

As he draws to a close, the author summons many kinds
of general counsels about how to live because 'the end of
all things is near' (v. 7). Early Christianity was lived
entirely under such a sign of urgency. The coming of the

end calls forth prayer, self-control, love ('because love covers over many sins', v. 8) and hospitality. Christians had to provide hospices and refuges for each other in a kind of network. They had to open their homes to each other, since they lacked church buildings or other formal centres. The author pictures that in the setting of love and hospitality the various members and leaders would bring special gifts. Verse 11 sounds very much like a conclusion to a sermon, a doxology, a benediction. With that 'Amen' it seems as if the service comes to an end. The rest of the letter has a more or less independent sound, though it repeats some now similar themes.

Suffering as a Christian

Of course, one may read this letter as a single document, penned by Peter or Silas, or someone speaking in Peter's name, without making any break at this point. But one may also choose to see this as a kind of appendix reflecting a somewhat later situation. The references to suffering in the earlier parts of the letter talk about futures, about opportunities to evade or minimize persecution when it comes. But now the present tense is used, 'My dear friends, do not be surprised at the painful test you are suffering' (v. 12). The persecution has now arrived, and it seems to have a formal and official character. But the writer does with this suffering what he had done with the foreseen or less regular trials mentioned earlier. He asks the Asian Christians to see that they are sharing Christ's sufferings, 'so that you may be full of joy when his glory is revealed' (v. 13).

People may suffer as criminals; Christians should not be among them. Suffering on those terms is humiliating, but just. If you suffer as a Christian, he says, there should be not shame but thankfulness and joy.

All this is written again under the sign of the end, the sense that 'the time has come for the judgement to begin, and God's own people are the first to be judged' (v. 17).

Judgement will be worse for those 'who do not believe the Good News from God'. This sense should motivate endurance in persecution, for right conduct in such trials and tests leads to trust in a Creator 'who always keeps his promise' (v. 19). It is hard to read this letter without being moved by the consistent, strong, undenying faith of its author.

The Flock of God

Whatever else the rest of this writing has been, the last chapter shows that it came in the form of a letter. The author addresses elders in the various congregations and asks them to work willingly and well. It seems strange to find Peter, or someone speaking for Peter, calling himself a fellow-elder, for his apostleship was a more dramatic role than eldership. But here may be a sign of humble identification. The elders are to work willingly. It is possible to picture people being reluctant even to be elders in a time of persecution. They might pretend to be too humble and modest, whereas they really wanted to escape responsibility. The opposite problem was also present. Some wanted to work for mere pay. After centuries of the existence of generally underpaid clergy it strikes modern Christian ears as strange to picture people going into church leadership for the sake of the pay. But the 'religion business' was big and tempting in the culture that surrounded the first Christians and may have lured them.

Now Christ, the example of leadership, is seen as the Chief Shepherd (v. 4) who offers a permanent crown.

Counsel to younger men to submit to their elders would be unsurprising to Jews or to most others of the day. The word of advice to them may have been necessary because of the temptations to pride that came to some converts. They must join others in wearing 'the apron of humility' (v. 5).

Most of all, the hard times called for alertness. The

Devil is pictured as a hungry lion; firm faith is needed for resistance. All this activity is lived in the light of a promise of eternal glory in union with Christ.

Final Greetings

Silas (sometimes referred to as Silvanus) may be the Silas of Acts 15 or some unknown figure who is described as the secretary, assistant, ghost writer, or agent of this writing. Babylon in verse 13 could very well be Rome.

'Greet each other with the kiss of Christian love. May peace be with all of you who belong to Christ' (v. 14). Thus ends a truly winning letter, a remarkable fragmentary record of early Christian existence. A eucharist or Lord's Supper – at which such a letter would be read – would quite naturally include the standard greeting of peace and love, the kiss. The author urges that behind that external sign the experience of Christ's peace be recognized by all. The tone of these last lines illustrates once more why in the twentieth century as in the first or second this letter inspires hope among Christian sufferers and calls forth witness when it is most difficult.

7. THE SECOND LETTER FROM PETER

After all the riches of 1 Peter, the writing that comes down to us as 2 Peter is quite a comedown. It needs little attention. Few Christians turn to it for Good News or for anything else, for that matter. It is probably the least read and least enjoyed material in the New Testament. Most scholars believe that it was the final document to be included and all of them know that 2 Peter 'barely made it' into the canon. Those who do not think Peter wrote it – and they include almost the entire scholarly community of no matter what persuasion – or the Christian readers who do not savour it as much as they do other writings, need have no bad conscience about seeing it as second-rate.

The letter seems to have been unknown and unregarded for a couple of centuries. When early lists of biblical canonical writings were prepared, 2 Peter rarely appeared. When it appeared, the faithful fathers dutifully reported that it was one of the 'spoken-against' or disputed books from the first. The conservative Protestant reformers let the classification *antilegomena*, spoken-against, stand – and did not base their teachings on it. Listen, thus, to Origen (185–254) as Eusebius quotes him: 'Peter has left one epistle generally acknowledged, and it may be a second; for there is a doubt about it.' Eusebius himself said, 'I recognize one epistle as genuine.' Centuries later, John Calvin thought it impossible for the true Peter to speak as negatively of Paul as does 2 Peter 3:15, 16 – but he did allow for the possibility that someone else wrote the letter at Peter's request.

Nothing in the style of 2 Peter lets it sound like the writings of the author of 1 Peter. The elegance is gone and a stiff, over-written, formal showiness prevails. The grand content of 1 Peter is not traceable here: no reference occurs to Jesus' death, resurrection, and ascension. The Holy Spirit is missing. Baptism is not referred to. Christian hope is not even hinted at. The author speaks of the apostles as being long gone, remembered figures of an ancient past (3:2), separated for generations from the author (3:4). For these reasons many date the letter as late as AD150.

Its value as a glimpse of early Christianity lies chiefly in the picture it gives of a church leader fighting off a heresy, perhaps something in the order of Gnosticism. That subject can be better treated when we take up the Johannine epistles. One item of curiosity: 1 Peter incorporates much of the material from the short letter of Jude. It is possible that both drew on a similar source, but most students believe that Peter simply incorporated and paraphrased the letter of Jude and made it his own.

The author takes pains to identity himself with Simon Peter (the original says Simeon, accenting the Jewishness of what is probably a writing from Jewish to Gentile Christians). Enough has been said about the questions this identification raises and the difficulty this letter had being accepted into the canon. Suffice it to say here that when we refer to Peter, it is possible to think of someone of a Petrine school, someone claiming Petrine authority.

Gods' Call and Choice

By the time of 2 Peter Hellenic ideas were very widely and deeply spread throughout much of the Christian community. The key words in this opening section reflect this, for they are Greek virtues: knowledge, self-control, endurance, godliness, brotherly love. There is nothing about them that is incompatible with Christian life, but they had to be appropriated and transformed, as the author does when he puts them in the context of faith and goodness. However secondary 2 Peter may have seemed to early Christians, they cannot have mistaken the announcement of Good News that breaks through it. Everything depends upon divine power and gifts, or promises and bonds with Jesus Christ.

The advice in verse 10 is appropriate, even where Good News comes as a gift. God has called and chosen, but the respondent has something to do with making these 'a permanent experience'. Because of the importance of this quest for permanence the author promises to keep on reminding readers of what they already know, of what has been 'firmly fixed in the truth you have received'. Where once truth and faith were fluid, dynamic, and almost unfinished, by the time of this writing they can be thought of as defined, entrenched, and static enough to be subjects for debate.

Peter here pictures himself as being near the point of death and is preparing for a new generation.

Eyewitnesses of Christ's Glory

The author promises to stick to the known outlines of Christ's life. His story squares with the one told in the gospels. Therefore he has credentials to repudiate 'made-up legends' (v. 16) – which were coming to be in abundance within decades – even as he certifies his presence at one of the events described in the gospels. The reference (vv. 16–17) is to the Transfiguration, where Peter, James, and John saw Jesus' appearance changed on a mountain top and heard the voice saying, 'This is my own dear Son, with whom I am well pleased!' He is eager to show that he heard the voice and saw Christ's greatness.

The experience made him confident of the prophetic message. This leads him to call his reader's attention to scriptural prophecy, and to the need for interpretation. People of that day often went to great lengths to read many meanings into and out of the Old Testament. The readers were surrounded by people who offered lavish but private interpretations which confused the faithful. Peter's call is not so much for church authority to explain Scriptures as for the call of the Holy Spirit, the same Spirit that brought the message from God through prophetic men.

False Teachers

While we know too little about the circumstances surrounding this letter, the middle chapter clearly shows why it was written. The entire section is a blast at false teachers who were true threats to the frail community. Whoever has had to deal with factionalism in any movement can sympathize with the author's concern. When the movement has to do with what its members conceived to be full truth and eternal life, the stakes are raised. The writer is not surprised that there are false teachers; he sees them as being in line with the false prophets that were predicted in Deuteronomy 13.

He points to four features of false leaders. First, they bring a party spirit by bringing in 'destructive . . . doctrines'. The word that they will 'bring in' such teaching suggests a subversive character. Second, they deny the Master who saved them (v. 1), literally, who 'purchased' or bought them – by then selling themselves to others. No one knows all of what is meant here, but there may have been some collusion between marginal Christians and rebellious Roman people who wanted power. They are, third, followers of 'immoral ways' who embarrass the Christians because non-Christians lump all those named as believers together. Thus they jeopardize the safety and strength of the Christian groups. And they are greedy, eager for profit (v. 3). Once again we learn of the dangers of the 'religion business' in the early Church.

The author takes these momentary disturbers of the peace and sees them in historic and cosmic contexts.

Verses 4–9 make up one crowded and unbroken sentence in the Greek; the author seems breathlessly eager to get his point across. He is influenced by a few words in Genesis 6 and many more in the non-biblical book of 1 Enoch. There we are told that 'angels who sinned' had to await judgement. Several Old Testament references come to his mind. First is the judgement on the old world in the Flood, a type of future judgement. Then there was the destruction of the sinful cities of Sodom and Gomorrah, against a prefigurement of final judgement. The reference to Lot as a good man should not be taken too seriously; he was at best comparatively good, since he had been shown in Genesis to be very weak. It is in apocryphal and other non-canonical literature that this positive picture of him was preserved. Here he serves as a reminder that Christians can escape punishment if they are godly.

2 Peter then describes false teachers as having bad personalities ('bold and arrogant', v. 10) and as being disrespectful of celestial beings, angels. Instinct rules their lives; but what is most dangerous is their participation in Christian rites, particularly the banquets or love-feasts. While they gorge, they also cause offence and confuse outsiders. Adultery is also on their mind. Most of all, they are in the business of leading in order to gain money. The writer refers here to Balaam as an example of such greed (Numbers 31). Balaam had been hired by a heathen ruler to draw the children of Israel into unfaithfulness. In Numbers 22:28 Balaam's donkey ('a dumb ass', v. 16) exposed his sin.

False teachers offered freedom, but produced slavery by leading baptized Christians back into their former errors – a worse situation than would have prevailed had they never come to Christ. They and their followers are like the unclean animals (to Jews), the dog and the sow; the proverb about the dog returning to his vomit (v. 22) is from Proverbs 26:11, though the source of the proverb about the pig is unknown. Comparing someone to dogs and pigs was as extreme an attack on another that a person of Jewish background at that time could make.

The Promise of the Lord's Coming

The opening verses of this last chapter show the author's eagerness to identify himself with Peter and the first letter of Peter. The early Church was evidently not convinced, and there has been some measure of suspicion about the book through most subsequent history. Because of what this chapter says about Paul, John Calvin did not think it could have come from the apostle Peter. Few modern students of the Bible can find a way to place it in the context of Peter's known time, ways, and outlook. Whoever wrote it, the chapter is interesting for the way the author regards his time and the future and the way he faces a particular problem occasioned by delay in Christ's second coming.

Of interest both in verse 2 and in verse 16 is the fact that by the time this letter was written, apostolic teaching is placed on a par with the Old Testament prophetic word – a novel and radical concept among those brought up in Judaism. Thus the author refers to Paul's letters as giving rise to problems for some people who then give a false explanation, 'as they do with other passages of the Scriptures'. But the greatest interest in the chapter derives from its particular way of discussing the end, the Day of the Lord, and Christ's second coming. If the scholars are correct in seeing 2 Peter as the last document to be included in the canon where it remained a 'disputed' book, then these are chronologically the last words in the Bible, even if they appear before the book of Revelation at the end of the book as we now have it.

The problem the author faced must have plagued Christians for decades. They had been passing around stories that Christ would soon return. If the gospels were in existence – and if this letter is of late date, 2 Peter reflects a world in which written gospels would be familiar – then both believers and non-believers would have access to promises of Christ's immediate return. Now the non-believers could come along and make fun of the followers: 'He promised to come, didn't he? Where is he? Our fathers have already died [a tell-tale clue that this is a late book], but everything is still the same as it was since the creation of the world!' (v. 4).

The author adopts several means to overcome their taunting. First, he reminds the readers that the world could end in several days. The original earth, 'formed out of water, and by water' (v. 5) – which is not a literal reading of Genesis – was destroyed by water at the time of the Flood. Now it would be destroyed again, in a second way, by fire. His second alternative is to introduce a new time-scale, one that may have given some explanation even if it was not finally satisfying. By reference to Psalm 90 we hear that 'in the Lord's sight' there is no difference 'between one day and a thousand years; to him the two are the same' (v. 8). Third, the delay represents God's willingness to be patient, to give people a chance to turn from their sins and be saved.

Jesus had referred to the suddenness and surprise of the Day of the Lord by comparing it to the coming of a thief in the night, and so does 2 Peter. He pictures an incandescent, melting universe – much as many modern physicists do. With such cosmic disorder and destruction in view, Christians should try to make the day come soon, for God has promised 'new heavens and a new earth'. They are to be pure and faultless and at peace with God for God's patience gives them an opportunity (v. 15).

Here follows the slightly uncomfortable reference to Paul, the peer or competitor of Peter for fame among early believers in the book of Acts and elsewhere. Paul wrote 'using the wisdom God gave him' (v. 15): this is kind of nervous compliment. 'There are some difficult things in his letters' is a true statement, but hardly necessary here. After the passing remarks about Paul comes one more warning against false teachers and one last plea that people would 'continue to grow' in Christ's grace and knowledge (v. 18).

8. THE LETTERS FROM JOHN

The three letters of John promote the Good News by working to ward off the Bad News. The Christian faith is not an agreement to a set of propositions or knowledge of a set number of doctrines. But while it centres in 'belief in', there are also examples of 'belief that' in the New Testament writings. And the apostles and evangelists also concerned themselves with the 'that'. In this particular instance, they saw a new and alternative set of teachings to be a total threat to the faith. So the author of these letters set out to do combat, to witness for the faith.

Church history has an unlovely word for this kind of activity. It is usually called 'heresy-hunting', and as such seldom has the ring of Good News about it. Over against orthodoxy or right teaching it poses heterodoxy, another teaching or heresy, a departure. The images of heresy-hunting are ugly. Those who study the New Testament at quiet desks, in bed, or around the family table do not like to have their serenity disturbed by recall of its brutalities. But there they are.

In the earliest Church the 'right teachers' fought heresy with argument and with tactics that excluded those unfortunate enough to deviate a bit. Three centuries later, when Christians of the Roman Empire came to possess the sword, they wasted little time using it against the very people who not long before had been persecuting them. In the Middle Ages the papacy scourged the heretics – Albigensians, Cathari, Waldensians – all bothersome sectarians who did not conform. They chased them to the mountain valleys or killed them. From the late Middle Ages the name of the Inquisition has survived as a symbol of forceful Christian insistence on truth and the killing of heretics. Lest Protestants become proud, they have to remember that in the name of the love of the Good News and its truth a John Calvin would assent to the killing of Servetus. In the New World, New England orthodox leaders banished sectarians.

Where force was not used, other kinds of pressures were almost as severe. Losers in ancient conciliar debates were often exiled; in the modern world, losers in denominational voting can become outcasts and can be purged. Matters of God's truth are decided by majority vote in conventions. Favoured teachers pursue innovators and experimenters. All this in the name of a faith that turned the world upside down. All this despite the fact that, as church historians regularly show us, it was as often as not the persecuted heretic who saw already what others did not see as yet – and who later came to be honoured as the true teacher over against the stuffy and often wrong defenders of the orthodox establishment. The history of Christian orthodoxy is in large part the recall of people who earlier had been called heretic.

Heresy-hunters come down to us through history as narrow, suspicious, self-righteous and arrogant people. The Christian faith is supposed to bring us peace. But the pursuers of heretics disturbed that peace. They would not know the Good News if it hit them head-on. Who did they think they were? We know pretty well who they were, thanks to modern psychological inquiries. They tended to be insecure people, unsure of their faith and themselves. They lashed out at people who threatened them. The American longshoreman and philosopher, Eric Hoffer, in *The True Believer*, made studies of the kind of people who sign up for True Faith and True Leader clubs. He noted quite properly that much orthodoxy is born not of a mutual love of truth among those who hold it but of a sense of mutual suspicion. No one trusts anyone, so they must impose standards and laws and punishments.

Well, the John of these letters is heresy-hunting. He

E

has no trouble hunting. The false teaching is now not only outside and around the congregations but within them, a threat to their vitals. He is fiery and fierce, sure of himself, exclusive and insistent. Yet we do not class him with the arrogant or the persecutors, the insecure or the suspicious. We look on these letters as the writings of one often called 'beloved', and think of them as controlled by the love of Christ and of fellow-human beings. The poet Robert Browning has said of John that he loved well because he hated well – he hated everything that stood in the way and the path of love. This author exposes his hatred of false teaching and his love of truth, and light, and love; of Christ and others.

In a way the need to make a point of the truth of the Good News is a compliment to the liveliness of the earliest Christian community. Where people are routine and apathetic it is hard for them to recognize issues in which truth and life are at stake. They drift and doze. But where movements are vital and outcomes uncertain, they have to argue. We picture the intense debates of revolutionaries in the America of 1776, the France of the 1790s, the Russia of 1917, as various factions and leaders set out to interpret the revolutionary acts and propose various scripts for the future. Why can't they get together? If they all got together, the momentum of their causes might well disappear. These letters were written when Christian faith was worth arguing about, when it had clear consequences for all of life.

What begins to separate the author of these letters from many subsequent definers and defenders is this: he had an unerring instinct for knowing what was a central and essential attack or assault. Much Christian love for truth has been compromised because the defenders of the faith get out the big artillery for little snipings. This kind of petty activity eventually wears the faithful down, so they can no longer even recognize when it is the core and heart of faith and life that is being threatened.

The point at issue in these letters and especially in the only one that goes on at enough length to cue us in, is 'the flesh of Jesus Christ'. That is the code-word for an enormously complicated debate. The author is disturbed by people who did not think that Jesus was the Christ or that in Christ God had taken on full humanity. 'This is how you will be able to know whether it is God's Spirit: anyone who declares that Jesus Christ came as a human being has the Spirit who comes from God. But anyone who denies this about Jesus does not have the Spirit from God. This spirit is from the Enemy of Christ' (1 John 4:2–3).

After nineteen centuries Christians may think that they can look back rather casually on that settled issue. But can they? I recall a theological professor some years ago commenting on a controversy during which pious people raged against the artistic portrayal of Jesus Christ in twentieth-century dress and in the company of the wrong kind of men and women. They did not complain that the artist who did the painting had been incompetent. They simply felt that Jesus should be kept from such taint. He should be seen as haloed and vaporous, gaseous and remote. The professor remarked: 'You will often find that among people who believe in Jesus Christ, his divinity will not be a difficult matter. It is the humanity that will trouble them. To picture him really as one of us, sweaty and troubled, weeping and enjoying himself at a boisterous wedding will be their problem.' It was hard to believe his words at that time. We were all well trained to defend the divinity of Christ. But it turns out that in Christian history and contemporary experience the *full* implications of his being one of us, our brother, at our side, sharing our life is bewildering, troublesome, and sometimes offensive teaching to Christians.

Without his taking on human flesh and sharing mortality the whole Good News is silenced, the whole New

Testament drama pointless. The letters of John show that, and make it their theme. Today when 'the new religions' of the occult and the metaphysical attract a new generation, it is interesting to note that most of them offer secret knowledge, a 'more spiritual' expression of religion, a more 'transcendental' experience.

We do not know in detail who was teaching what these letters condemn, but it is not hard to reconstruct the false teaching from these letters and from what else was going on at that time. Picture three concentrics. The outer or most general is called 'Gnosticism'. This philosophy was a part of the *Zeitgeist*, the 'climate of opinion', the spirit of the times. It came to people as naturally as 'breathing out and breathing in'. Gnostics were dualistic, separating spirit from matter and despising matter. Salvation was saving people out of matter. Salvation occurred through participating in mysterious rites and by acquiring special and usually secret superior knowledge. Through these one became godlike.

Within Gnosticism and its denial of the body and of matter there developed, secondly, a special kind of Christian version, usually called Docetism, which has sometimes been translated as 'Seemism'. The body is bad; matter is to be shrugged off. The flesh cannot house true spirit. Then what shall become of Jesus of Nazareth? Well, he only seemed to have a body, to be a human. The true and pure follower could go beyond following his body, to the realms of true spirit. By the way, Docetism allowed for two moral extremes. The one was a denial of the good things of life because they were material. The other allowed adherents to be libertines, because material things – from the realm in which one over-indulged and sinned – did not have real meaning for believers.

We also know, thirdly, that at the end of the first century in Asia Minor a false teacher named Cerinthus presented his own adaptation of Gnosticism-Docetism. One amusing and illuminating anecdote from early church history has the aged apostle John unwilling even to enter a bath-house in which Cerinthus was bathing for fear the roof would fall in on such a false teacher! Cerinthianism *may* have been the point of attack in this letter.

The author of this letter did not wait for roofs to fall in. He went on the attack in the name of the Good News that Christ was the incarnate and enfleshed Son of God, one with humans, and that the tests of faith and life occurred in our real world. He does all this in the setting of truth, life, and love: 'This is what love is: it is not that we have loved God, but that he loved us and sent his Son to be the means by which our sins are forgiven. Dear friends, if this is how God loved us, then we should love one another' (1 John 4:10–11). Here is Good News stated as forcefully and forthrightly as in the gospel that also bears the name of John.

How he fights heresy separates John from most of his errant successors in that role. He never forgets what he is about and why he pursues it. He does not get lost in his ego, in the self-centredness of his own creed. The letter is rather unstructured. Those who try to outline it usually despair of the project. But certain marks stand out. It is most of all pastoral. The author is quite assuredly a very aged man. He has seen much and endured much. The final crisis of history might be present in this struggle against the Enemy or Anti-Christ. Never mind. While he can be impassioned, he can also be calm, never losing control. He does not name names. He does not drive the weak into the camp of the enemy but tries to win them over to complete commitment to the love of God in his Christ. So his writing is essentially positive, designed to unite the faithful. His strength lies also in his love for the congregation. The lovers of false teaching are exclusivist, snobbish, eager to authenticate their own virtues and experiences, ready to set their own ethical patterns. They represent a falling-away. Whoever has

endured exclusivist Gnostics in a contemporary congregation knows how disruptive they can be. But these letters
keep trying to restore unity. The effort comes to a climax
in 1 John 4:7–21, which is often called the greatest
hymn to love in the New Testament – certainly a match
for 1 Corinthians 13. But these writings do not only soar;
they are also practical. The tests of truth are in the doing.
Loving God and hating the neighbour are incompatibles.
Christian faith can be seen in love, in the overcoming of
sin.

The second and third letters of John do not demand
much separate treatment. Most commentators think they
came from the same hand as 1 John, but are a bit more
focused, provincial, and even narrow. The author may
become a bit too tough for many tastes in 2 John. In
verses 9–10 he seems almost to be repudiating anyone
who talks about or yearns for change and progress.
Is 'the elder' growing too old? Why must he even forbid
hospitality to the deviants? In a sense, 2 John is written
in the mood of Edmund Burke's line: if it is not necessary
to change, it is necessary not to change.

The big change has come with the Big News, and people
who want to change that by denying the flesh of Christ are
too threatening to be granted a Christian greeting. 3
John centres on a dispute over authority, and is also less
to the taste of those who thirst for Good News than is 1
John. Whether the other writings are first drafts, specific
applications, or follow-ups to the first letter, they add
little, though what is positive in them grows out of its
viewpoint.

We can never know enough to satisfy our curiosity
about the audiences and authors of these letters, and are
given only tantalizing glimpses. Most scholars ancient
and modern – the great British scholar C. H. Dodd is a
rare but important exception – believe that they were
written by the author of the Fourth Gospel, though his
name, 'John', appears only in the title of the books and

never in the books themselves. Those who believe that
'the Beloved Disciple' named John, the son of Zebedee,
wrote the Fourth Gospel – and most readers from the
early centuries to the nineteenth had no doubts about
that – will then see this same John as the author of these
letters named after him. They then have to picture him
as a very, very old man when these were written – well
into his nineties – and have to account for the fact that
this apostle also called himself 'the elder'.

Others use the author's self-chosen name, the Elder,
as a designation. They picture him at Ephesus in Asia
Minor, a man at home in the Greek thought-world,
writing to people who shared that world. The strengths
of the Fourth Gospel and many of its phrases, contrasts,
and cadences, mark 1 John. Whoever he was, Beloved
Disciple or Ephesian Elder, he is at the heart of the matter
so far as Christian faith is concerned. Whenever someone
is tempted to offer superior knowledge, a morality that
goes beyond what is available to all of us, a faith that
never touches ground or flesh or body, these writings
will be consulted to remind believers that their faith is
to be known and tested and touched in our bodily and
natural worlds. Archbishop William Temple has called
Christianity the most materialist of all the great religions.
Martin Thornton reminds Christians that at least a loaf
of bread, a bottle of wine, and a river are needed for its
full expression. These letters show what Good News it
is that God has chosen to condescend to humans' ways,
to take on their conditions, to impart and exact a love
they can experience and embody.

9. THE FIRST LETTER FROM JOHN

The Word of Life

The first letter of John begins with no reference to John or anyone else as letter-writer, and no one is named as author anywhere in the text. More strikingly, the writer does nothing to make this look like a letter. It is a kind of tract, an expounding of the faith. But if there is no greeting, there is a preface. Whoever knows the Bible at all will know something of the prologue to the Fourth Gospel (John 1:1–14) and cannot help but hear reminiscences of it in the first four verses of this writing.

The grandeur is there. Much of the sweep of the Gospel's prologue can at least be remembered as one reads these words about the Word of life. The author stakes out a territory and a position that he will defend against all comers – and there are plenty of them. He is going to locate the Good News in the plot of human history, almost to rub the noses of those who would keep Jesus Christ off in a world of cloudlands and shadows, mists and ideas. This is going to be a message about a heard, seen, touched Christ. That is clear enough.

Almost nothing else about the preface is clear. These introductions to the Good News are not designed to be point-for-point commentaries on the original texts, so rarely need they refer to difficulties of translation. But these verses represent such a classic case of difficulty that to dwell on the subject for a moment might serve to remind the reader of the problems faced by translators and commentators. These first verses have been universally seen as an almost hopeless grammatical tangle, one that cannot be straightened out to everyone's satisfaction, one that must inspire some guesses about the author's true meaning. C. H. Dodd has translated the

Greek word for word. It comes out like this:

> That which was from the beginning; that which we
> have heard; that which we have seen with our eyes;
> that which we observed and our hands felt – con-
> cerning the Word of life – and the life was manifested,
> and we have seen and bear witness and announce
> to you the eternal life which was with the Father and
> was manifested to us – that which we have seen and
> heard we announce to you also.

Now read the more clear lines in the current translation
and you will have an idea of the trials of interpreters.

Too much can be made of the difficulties. The general
idea is clear. John refers to the Word of life, for which the
Greek word was *logos*. *Logos* means 'word' or 'speech'
or 'reason' or 'reasoned utterance'. While in the Fourth
Gospel the term appears alone, here it is connected with
'of life', and sets readers up for the theme of the epistle,
in which *logos* never reappears but 'life' is frequent.
The phrase has been translated 'the revelation of life',
or 'the Gospel', but we might even be more precise and
say that he is here referring to the Good News of life
in Christ.

That Good News has existed from the beginning. But
in the face of those who denied the Word of life as the
story of the earthly Jesus, the author, also eager to
establish his credentials or to tie himself in with the experience of the young Church, says 'we have heard it . . .
yes, we have seen it, and our hands have touched it'
(v. 1). It is not always easy to know when John is using
'we' and 'our' as a sign of modesty to replace the singular,
or when he uses what is today called an editorial 'we'.
Most often he seems to be speaking of the combined
experience of the original Christian community. He
insists: this life became visible. While the Gospel wants
to connect the eternal Word with the Jesus who lived

among men, the epistle preface wants doubters to know
that he who was seen and known 'was with the Father'
(v. 2).

The purpose of his writing is 'so that you will join with
us in the fellowship' and 'in order that our joy may be
complete' (vv. 3–4). When church membership has become
something automatic in a culture, or implies only the act
of signing a parish's constitution, a linking-up with
'the church of your choice', much of the sense of the
original fellowship is lost. The Greek word *koinonia*
talks of profound sharing and shareholding, the pooling
of resources and destinies, the abandonment of one's
own prerogatives and sometimes of one's property, in
order that the sense of mutual dependence be stronger
and isolation minimized. When such fellowship existed,
little wonder that joy would be complete.

God Is Light

Nowhere else in the New Testament is God called light.
'God is light.' There are no qualifiers. The phrase is clear
and absolute. Such an idea was common in certain styles
of Greek philosophy, but it is also not out of line at all
with themes in the Old Testament. Christ does not ever
speak in such simple terms of identification, but it is
not wrong for John to say that this message 'we have
heard from his Son.' He is not interested here in writing
a textbook of Christian philosophy but in moving
instantly to the moral claims that go with this statement.
It is the nature of God to reveal himself as it is the nature
of light to shine. If God has shone into our world and
'yet at the same time [we] live in the darkness', then we
are not in fellowship with him as we claim, and 'we are
lying in our words and in our actions' (v. 6). A phrase
here can be translated, if 'we do not the truth'. 'Doing
the truth' is a good Jewish concept of ethics, carried
over into Johannine versions of Christianity. Truth is

not simply 'true statements', but reliability or faithfulness, and 'doing the truth' is practising such faithfulness in our goodness.

The phrase 'if we say' is the first in a sequence of parallels. Readers can picture the author in debate with the enemies, the non-doers of truth. They offer several false interpretations. First is their willingness to deny that sin or evil break human fellowship with God or that good action does not matter. The breakaway group says in effect that they enjoy fellowship with God, but they do not care about right living. John argues that wickedness is darkness, and if there is a trace of darkness in a life, it blots and blocks the life of God. Nowhere else in the letter is the author as clear about the Good News as he is in the reponse on this point: living in the light means fellowship with one another 'and the blood of Jesus, his Son, makes us clean from every sin' (v. 7).

The second 'if we say' shows the schismatic group's saying that sin does not exist in their nature, that they have moved beyond sinfulness. But 'if we say that we have no sin, we deceive ourselves and there is no truth in us' (v. 8). The Gnostic heretics spoke in these terms. Enlightened and knowledgeable members of the cult had moved past the realm where moral charges could be made against them. John would counter this with the Christian idea of confessing sins, trusting in God, and receiving forgiveness.

The third says, 'If we say that we have not sinned . . .' (v. 10). We can almost hear the voice of his enemies here. They will not admit that sin is evident in their way of life, that they have sinned. Some people might have, but we, the 'in' group, have not. John cannot live with this, for it makes God a liar. He has told us that all sinned. Why else would he have sent Christ but for our sins? There is no room in the Christian fellowship for the person who considers himself or herself a part of a special group of people who can make special claims on God or virtue. All are equally in need, equally dependent upon God.

Christ Our Helper

The writer is aged, or he wants to establish a fatherly intimacy, for he refers to the recipients of his epistle as 'my children', even though we must picture many of them as having reached beyond maturity. The endearing phrase is part of his call to them to refrain from sin. He does not want evil to be taken casually. But he is writing Good News also to those who admit that they do sin, so he must depict and offer the remedy. 'If anyone does sin, we have Jesus Christ, the righteous, who pleads for us with the Father' (v. 1). 'Pleads for us' grows out of the word that is sometimes translated 'paraclete'. In the Fourth Gospel the paraclete is the Holy Spirit, but here it refers directly to Christ. A paraclete is an advocate, but more than the lawyer's sense of the term is meant. He is called to the side of someone to make the case.

John goes on to say that 'Christ himself is the means by which our sins are forgiven' (v. 2). The Greek word interpreted by the phrase 'the means by which our sins are forgiven' is *hilasmos*; it appears twice in this letter and nowhere else in the New Testament. The word has virtually disappeared from the modern vocabulary. As scholars debate whether 'propitiation' or 'expiation' best serves, the rest of us reach for our dictionaries and, having read them, still do not know what exactly is meant. The pagans had a concept of propitiation which they connected with the idea of bringing offerings to appease angry deities. Moderns can picture how this kind of idea could have crept into Christian interpretations, given their inherited understandings of God's wrath and of humans' sacrifice. Whereas pagan deities' wrath was often random, God's is pictured as being inspired by his nature as the creator of justice and mercy alike. But he does not need to be appeased. He begins the process

of changing relations with humans. No human gift or
event changes God's way of dealing with people. Christ's
loving self-offering does. Therefore it is perfectly proper
to translate the phrase as here. Christ is the means through
which God acts to forgive our sins.

The argument with the heretics is picked up again.
'If someone says, "I do know him," but does not obey
his commands, such a person is a liar and there is no
truth in him' (v. 4). The moral test is obedience to God.
The people who were giving the Church trouble claimed
special experiences, special knowledge. Why should they
be troubled with moral action? The response is that
knowing God brings with it obedience. Christ is the
model for this way of acting.

The New Command

The writer is concerned with the command to love. He
speaks of it as being an old command, because believers
have long known it. But it is also new, because in Christ
the old darkness is passing away. This sets him up for
another imaginary encounter with a heretic. This one
is the teacher who says he 'is in the light, yet hates his
brother'. Hatred belongs to darkness, to the old. With
the themes now established, the letter provides two little
essays or addresses, one to the Church and one about
the world.

To the Church, John uses six little phrases, each beginning with 'I write' or, just to vary things – and probably
not to refer back to earlier writing – 'I have written.'
The current translation, to keep from confusion but at
the expense of permitting repetition, uses 'I write' all
six times. Twice the author addresses 'my children', who
are probably beginners in faith. Twice he addresses
'fathers', who represent maturity and fulfilment in the
congregations. And twice he speaks to the young men,
who in the prime of life are developing in faith and power.
The six little addresses add nothing new to the content

of the letter, but they do reinforce and personalize its themes.

About the world: his essay on the world, verses 15–17, sounds wholly negative. The world represents the sinful self and its desires. This is not the only way to think of the world. In the Fourth Gospel God so loved the world that he gave his Son. There the world was the sphere or arena of his action, and was not to be despised. There is much love of the world in this epistle, too. But not when the world is seen as under the domain of the Evil One, as thwarting the purposes of God. That world 'and everything in it that men desire is passing away' (v. 17). John is not so much here pleading for crabby, world-denying people as seeking to help form people who see beyond the world's momentary pleasures to the eternal purposes of God.

The Enemy of Christ

After two little side words about Church and world the author returns to his main theme. He has already shown that the test of truth and light is moral and social. Now he sees it as theological or doctrinal. 'The end is near!' (v. 18). This is not a novel teaching. The whole New Testament is written under the mark of its urgency. The author uses strange logic to make his point. The people were told that the Enemy of Christ would come. Many enemies have appeared. So they know the time is near. This letter speaks of an Anti-Christ, some historical figure to be associated with the end time. But the anti-Christs were any who did not have the spirit of Christ; they never really did belong 'to our group' (v. 19). Now they are gone. Those who have the Holy Spirit 'poured out' (v. 27) will know the truth. The enemy of the truth is the Enemy of Christ, the one who says that Jesus is not the Christ. This denial is also a denial of the Father. The author's concern is not so much to give a complete description of Christian teaching as to provide some slogans, some touchstones which can be used to identify false teaching. Here the stress on the Spirit is strong: there is real confidence that the Spirit will teach rightly all who remain in Christ and in the community.

Children of God

When John comes to talk about the dangers of sin he comes forth with a startling concept: the believers are children of the Father and they are therefore like him. Well and good, but he is not a sinner, and this letter has condemned all who claim that they are not sinners. When the author elaborates his teaching on this subject, he seems to come out in flat contradiction against what he has taught in the first chapter. It is necessary to see his argument unfold.

'See how much the Father has loved us!' (v. 1). He begins on a rhapsodic note, for he tries to impart a sense of a valid heritage to the Christian community. 'In fact, we are' God's children. The world cannot see this and has no means of recognizing it because it has not known God. John then throws things into the future. He pictures Christ's future appearing – the word suggests the visit of a head of state or an important person with presence. When that occurs, believers shall become like him. John does not announce all this in order to impart a new doctrine but to inspire a new ethic: 'Everyone who has this hope in Christ keeps himself pure, just as Christ is pure' (v. 3). They are to be modelled after what they shall become.

John speaks three times to the issue of sin, ringing variations or changes on one theme. First is a negative reference to sin as a breaking of God's law. Sin means many different things in the Bible. To today's world it often means being a bit weak, blurring a line between right and wrong, expressing a frailty, not coming up to standard, or making an error of judgement. John will have none of that. He is a dark-and-light, nothing-or-all thinker. Every sin is a violation of God's highest intentions for humans. Christ is again the model. There is no sin in him. Whoever lives in Christ, then, will not continue to sin.

The second is a positive statement. The author flips over his previous assertion. 'Whoever does what is right is righteous, just as Christ is righteous' (v. 7). Here the opposite of God's or Christ's purity is introduced in the form of the Devil, who 'has sinned from the very beginning' (v. 8). Whoever sins, then, has nothing of God in him, and is of the Devil. Moderns are not accustomed to thinking in terms of such a cosmic drama when they or those near them falter or fail. Yet in certain moments in history people are capable of resurrecting such language. During the Nazi period, people otherwise unmoved by Christian language sometimes found it necessary to speak in terms of the demonic. They saw a mode of existence that was incapable of doing anything but destroy. They almost heard the wing-beat of demonic forces, so vivid were these. To the early Christians the enemies both without and within posed threats to the fragile community. To understand them, one needed extraordinary explanations and the figure of the Devil was a natural choice.

The third expression is one that has inspired much comment. Recall 1 John 1:8: 'If we say that we have no sin, we deceive ourselves and there is no truth in us.' Now John writes (v. 9), 'Whoever is a child of God does not continue to sin . . . he cannot continue to sin.' The translation minimizes the shock of apparent contradiction by introducing the words 'continue to' or 'continue in' as a means of noting the fact that something is different between chapters one and three. The tenses are. By this choice of term the translator is making his own commitment as to how to resolve the difficulty. The Greek language offers subtle distinctions between times and modes of action, as expressed in verb forms. The form used here does suggest habitual, continued action. The author could then be saying that while no one dare claim that he or she never sins, to be children of the Father and modelled after Christ is to leave behind habitual sinning.

Apparent conflicts like those between these two chapters or verses keep people in the commenting business active. Many other explanations have been offered. Some say that the author is not picturing Christians as they are in the flesh and in reality but as they should ideally be. That approach is not too satisfying in John's world. Others say that since the Christ-like life does produce a measure of purity, this Johannine ideal becomes ever more realistic in the life of the Christian. We have read interpreters saying that the sin here referred to is of the outrageous and visible kind. But the text does not say that. It has been argued that God uses a different standard in judging what is sin in the life of one who is his child. But sin is sin. He may, according to the Scriptures, *do* different things about his children's sins than about others, but he does not have a different regard for some kinds of sins over against others. Could the elder be referring to the two sides of believers' natures? The child-of-God side is sinless, but when God regards believers apart from their inheritance, they remain sinners. Some biblical texts do indeed suggest this, but that is not the current point.

The best explanation, or half an explanation, is probably locked into the subtlety of the grammar here, in the distinction between habitual sin and acts of sin, between a state of mind that persistently leads to evil and the spirit of sonship. This interpretation may be giving a great deal of credit to the feel for language of those first readers. It may also be pointed out that this writer, like many others, uses extreme language for whatever point he is making. He is not fighting off a different heresy from that in chapter one. He is interested in pointed moral counsel and not in logical neatness.

Love One Another

The fact that we are children of God leads us, says John, to love. Here follows one of the favourite and yet one of the most threatening sections in the letter. Hymns to love are central to the Good News. Sooner or later they converge on the perfect example and enactment of love. 'This is how we know what love is: Christ gave his life for us' (v. 16). It is by now well known in the Christian community that the Greek had different words for love. Some of them implied care, some friendship, some self-love (erotic, and the like). But the cherished word is *agape* (a-gah-pay), which refers to unmotivated, spontaneous, free, self-giving love. This love, John keeps saying, is the kind the Father had to have for humans, since there was nothing in sinful people that would have inspired God to deal with them as being attractive. Instead of finding the object of his love, he created it, by sending Christ to be identified with humans and to become human.

The announcement of such Good News is also always comforting. But it brings some corollaries which may be less soothing. 'We too, then, ought to give our lives for our brothers!' That sounds like high drama, remote from ordinary life. But Christian history is rich in examples of precisely such love. In case the drama and the ideal seem too high and noble for the rest of us, the author continues with a kind of let-down, descending to our regular world. He says that if we close our hearts against a brother in need when we have possessions, we cannot claim to have love for God in our hearts.

Some readers may detect a slight narrowing of love in this letter. In the gospels disciples are to love all people, especially including their neighbour in need and their enemy. Now the accent is on loving 'the brother'. The two ideas are, of course, not mutually exclusive. Love begins at home. The test of love may be first with those closest. If it cannot exist there, it will exist nowhere. The intimate sphere is a good practice ground for a larger exercise of love. Second, in John 15:12 Christ had also commanded such love among his followers. The purpose of this letter also has to be remembered. The author could point to false leaders who were not showing love while they claimed they were Christians. But the same letter probably also reflects a condition in which the lines between the congregation and the outside world were being more decisively drawn. If they do not love each other, the letter seems to say, they will not receive much love because the world will not care. Talk of love is important, but 'our love should not be just words and talk; it must be true love, which shows itself in action' (v. 18).

Courage before God

Verses 19–20 are very difficult and tangled verses in the original Greek. From the earliest times Christian commentators had difficulty about their interpretation, especially with the word that is translated 'our hearts *will be confident* in God's presence' (v. 19). After everything has been sorted out and clarified, two main readings survive. The first sees it as a warning. 'But in his presence we shall [do well to] convince our heart that, if even our own heart condemn us, God is greater than our heart and knows everything.' The alternative – here I am following a reading offered by Neil Alexander – is a comfort. 'And in his presence we shall reassure our heart, whenever our heart condemn us; because God is greater than our heart and knows everything.' The first would be severe. Don't assure yourself too readily that you love in truth and are of truth. Your own heart teaches you to question your own sincerity, and God knows more than

does your heart. The second reading is: do not lose
heart over your failures. God knows them: he knows all
about human frailty, but he knows that you basically
belong to him and, in spite of your failures, he knows
you will be found with him. Alexander favours the
second version and quotes another interpreter, A. E.
Brooke: 'The aim of the whole passage is surely to give
assurance, and not to strike terror into their [the readers']
hearts.' Our translation supports such an understanding.

Love is seen as a command. God commands that people
believe 'in the name of his Son Jesus Christ and love one
another, just as Christ commanded us.' God has given
the Spirit, so we can know God lives in us (vv. 23–24).

The True and the False Spirit

The early Christian world presented a mixture of godliness and godlessness, religiousness and what today we
would call secularity. Some people had faith in nature
and in laws, or simply turned their backs on claims of
diverse powers. But most of them were very much taken
up with spirits and deities. The Christian community
was not wholly able to be divorced from the spirit of
the times, the *Zeitgeist*. Tough-minded letters like this
one were designed to help them keep a distance.

In that Christian community as we know from instances in the book of Acts and in Paul's letters to the
Corinthians, people were often given over to ecstatic
and extravagant expressions. Some of them spoke in
unknown tongues, or went into trances, or made extraordinary claims for their supernatural powers. Today
some extreme elements in the charismatic or Jesus
movements blend with some occult groups. In that climate,
the author seems to be saying, do not assume that everything religious is superior to its alternatives or that
everything spiritual is Christian.

Many false prophets had gone out everywhere. Did we
not know of the volatility and eccentricity of these, we

would be tempted to sense a tinge of paranoia in writers like John. But he keeps his head and asks that those who claim the Spirit should be tested. In his present circumstance, facing a specific heresy, this meant that they should discern whether the prophet 'declares that Jesus Christ came as a human being'. If he does not he 'does not have the Spirit from God' (vv. 2–3).

The next paragraph sounds prideful. 'You belong to God . . . and have defeated the false prophets.' 'We belong to God.' Once again, the either/or language is pushed to its limit. The author is trying to point to objective ways of telling true prophets from false ones rather than establish reasons for egocentrism among himself and his 'children'.

God Is Love

The climax of this epistle comes with this essay on love. There are no particular textual difficulties, and a commentator or introducer may be best advised to say as little as possible, and then get out of the way so that the text can work its effects on a new generation. Those familiar with it often cherish it alongside 1 Corinthians 13. It also echoes parts of the Fourth Gospel; verse 9 seems to derive from John 3:16: 'This is how God showed his love for us: he sent his only Son into the world that we might have life through him.'

God is love, which is not quite the same thing as saying love is God! This has been said and read and heard so often that its shock value has all but disappeared. But when John made this theological assertion – stronger than it is made anywhere else in Scripture, and made twice in this letter – he was countering and bypassing most ancient definitions of God and trying to stamp one clear idea in his listeners' or readers' minds. But his purpose, as so often, is ethical. God has placed the neighbour or the brother visibly in our way. Not to love him but to claim to love God makes one a liar and one who does not know God.

The accent falls on the need that 'we should love one another.' Our love is derivative, a channelling of God's love. *Agape* means not that we have loved God, but that he loved us and sent his Son to be the means by which our sins are forgiven (v. 10). The Good News almost comes in capsules at this point in the letter. As so often, the author also points ahead toward what is now called 'Judgement Day'. Courage for it will come from our having lived in love, 'because our life in this world is the same as Christ's' (v. 17). For that reason love of the brother is the example, the test, the taste, the foretaste of God's complete self-giving love in Christ as grasped in Christian community.

Our Victory over the World

The Bishop of Leicester, R. R. Williams, commenting on 5:1, says that it would have been nice if the letter read, 'By this we know that we love God and keep his commandments, when we love the children of God.' But what has come down to us is, literally, 'In this we know that we love the children of God whenever we love God.' Did the writer become a bit tangled, or did an early copyist make a mistake? Our translation tries to make clear sense. 'Whoever believes that Jesus is the Messiah is a child of God; and whoever loves a father loves his child also.' The New English Bible has it: 'to love the parent means to love his child.'

At this point many a reader must have felt as the author could picture his earliest readers feeling: all this is too much for us. We do not keep the commandments. We do not embody perfect love. We fail the brothers. We make false claims. We do not live up to the commandment of love. How, then, can we be God's children? Because, he suddenly inserts, 'his commands are not too hard for us, because every child of God is able to defeat the world' (v. 4). Jesus is also pictured as saying that his yoke is easy, his burden is light. The Sermon on the Mount is hard and strong stuff, but the command to love is not burdensome or defeating. Three times the author speaks of 'defeating the world', reinforcing the point that belief in Jesus as the Son of God is an equipping power that brings victories.

The Witness about Jesus Christ

No one knows for sure to what the writer was referring when (v. 6) he said that Jesus Christ 'came with the water of his baptism and the blood of his death. He came not only with the water, but with both the water and the blood.' Some have seen in water and blood a reference to both Baptism and the Lord's Supper. With probably more plausibility some have pointed to the passage in John 19:34 where the witness – quite possibly the same author – insists that blood and water flowed from Christ's side. We could be more sure of what he is saying if we knew the details of the heresy he was countering.

The best surmise is that the Cerinthians taught that the Christ came only into the human Jesus at his baptism, but that the Christ was no longer part of Jesus at the crucifixion. No, the Christ died when Jesus died. 'Blood' here simply certifies the fact of his death. The Spirit, probably the Holy Spirit, serves as additional witness. The whole passage is written to lead to the concept of eternal life as a gift that comes with 'having' the Son of God.

Eternal Life

The letter's close includes three affirmations. None of them are surprises to anyone who has read what has gone before. After summary comment on eternal life, courage, and prayer, we hear first that 'no child of God keeps on sinning' (v. 18). Second, 'We know that we belong to God even though the whole world is under the rule of the Evil One.' Here is a dividing-line theology that is implied throughout the letter. There is no middle ground between the two families of man. Third, 'We know that the Son of God has come' (v. 20) – a word that leads to the closing sentence, verse 21, 'My children, keep yourselves safe from false gods!' We do not know whether these were the blatant idols of a pagan world or the somewhat more subtle alternatives to the knowledge of God in Christ. In either case, the author asks why people should settle for less than full light, truth, and love, and he does this asking in the form of a tender warning to the people whom he has throughout called 'my children'.

10. THE SECOND AND THIRD LETTERS FROM JOHN

The Second Letter

The second letter adds little interest or substance to the message of 1 John. Much speculation has been raised about the opening address, 'From the Elder – To the dear Lady and to her children.' Many have seen in the 'dear' or 'elect' Lady phrase a reference to a particular individual. It is not possible to prove that the author could not have had one in mind, but in verse 13 he refers to 'your dear Sister' by the same name. It is not likely for two sisters to have identical names. Nor is the universal or 'catholic' Church the recipient of this letter, because, as has often been pointed out, that Church has no 'sister'. Most readers have come to think of the dear Lady as a local congregation, personified in feminine form just as today nations, ships, and other entities are sometimes treated.

Two noteworthy accents appear. First, there is a general hardening of position accompanied by a change in tone, after the first letter. The author is now even more sure of himself, more convinced that the 'deceivers' need opposition. The second is a specific policy associated with his charge that they avoid heresy. The false teacher is not even to be welcomed to a home with the greeting, 'Peace be with you.' It would be unwise and not fully biblical to establish a universal Christian policy on the basis of this abrupt and rude counsel. The heretical threat was subtle *and* total. In this specific situation the author counselled what few in the New Testament, including Jesus himself, would do: to end conversation, dialogue, debate, efforts to continue communication. Evidently false teachers were having some success at insinuating themselves into people's homes or assemblies and winning them away. For that time and place the counsel of avoidance was in order, as it may occasionally be in our own time.

Tucked into the paragraph is one other idea that has caught some attention. Verse 9 says that 'anyone who does not stay with the teaching of Christ, but goes beyond it, does not have God.' The idea of 'staying with' past teaching has helped produce static dogmatisms, claims that the Church dare not develop new and expanding ways to affirm the life of God in Christ. This is not the only word to be said on the subject of such development; the New Testament itself shows certain measures of it. The key here is the idea that one cannot and dare not go beyond the teaching of Christ, who offers God to humans. The corral that the author stakes out here is large, for Christ is the encompassing truth.

The Third Letter

The third letter differs entirely from the other two, in that it is addressed to an individual, Gaius, and it refers by name to two leaders, Diotrephes and Demetrius. Gaius is known only from these few lines. The author has heard good reports from people who came to Gaius as strangers. They were aided by him, and he demonstrated his love for the Church. So John can ask him for more help as missioners come by 'on their journey in the service of Christ'. It was a point of pride among the early Christian leaders that they would not accept any help from pagans. This added to the responsibility of fellow-believers.

The other letters of John give almost no pictures of the actual life of young congregations except that they were plagued by heretics. Now we finally come face to face with a situation and are told less than we would like. The Greek text calls Diotrephes 'their loving-to-take-the-lead Diotrephes'. Some have seen here the beginnings of a dispute between an elder and a 'bishop', a single leader who has an authority rightfully gained but misuses it. The author does not accuse him of false teaching but of bad manners, personal likes, lack of hospitality. The early Church was not a Golden Age, it did not leave us 'good old days' for looking back on. Paul opposed Peter and had other fallings-out. The disciples were often jealous of each other. Here may have been a personality clash, a petty dispute, an argument over the styles and forms of church government.

Were Diotrephes clearly guilty of false teaching, one would expect the elder to accuse him, but he does not. Of course, we cannot be sure there was not also a theological dispute behind the clash. We only learn that Diotrephes looks ambitious and power-mad to the elder and will not pay any attention to what the author said in a previous 'short letter' (v. 9) – could it have been the second letter of John?

Gaius, at least, is not to imitate the bad but the good. Speaking of the good, John says, there is Demetrius. 'Everyone speaks well' of him; 'truth itself speaks well of him'; the elder even speaks well of him, 'and you know that what we say is true' (v. 12).

The letter ends as did 2 John, with nothing particularly original or elevating – just an expression that there is more to say. Most of us often end our letters the same way, speaking of the press of time, the frustration of using written greetings, the desire to see others in person. In 2 John the author refers to 'paper and ink' and now to 'pen and ink' (v. 13). The subtle variation is often regarded as a tell-tale trace of common authorship. Had someone been forging an additional letter, he might well have stuck to the formula. 'Greet all our friends personally' (v. 15): did the elder have an 'inner circle' of closer friends in the larger congregation? There is no reason to read anything cliquish into such an innocent line. Here is an author who searches and reaches for personal contact and seeks literary forms that come close to expressing it.

11. THE LETTER FROM JUDE

Jude ranks with 2 Peter among the final writings to be included in the New Testament. The 456-word tract is focused against false teaching; it exhorts believers to be loyal and to stand against heresies. Verses 17–19 suggest that prophecies of the apostolic period have already been fulfilled – a hint that much time has elapsed before this writing. In that case, the book is not of apostolic authorship. It is one of the writings that were disputed or 'spoken against' from the first, when the canon was forming. It lives more as a curiosity, a point of information about how early Christians faced and feared deviant teaching, than as an embodiment of Good News.

The author claims to be a brother of James. 'Jude, a servant of Jesus Christ, and the brother of James' (v. 1), but he does not say which James it is, and the tradition that finds him a brother of the brother of Jesus has little foundation. We know nothing much about him. Jude did appear in the Muratorian Canon, a listing of New Testament books that dates from AD190 and is referred to by a number of the fathers. His letter went to 'those who have been called by God' and not to a particular congregation.

Lest any reader get the idea that 2 Peter and Jude, probably the last two books to be written and to be incorporated into the canon, have no value beyond the historical, we should remind them that one of the most beautiful benedictions or sign-offs in the Bible concludes this letter: 'To him who is able to keep you from falling and bring you faultless and joyful before his glorious presence – to the only God our Saviour, through Jesus Christ our Lord, be glory, majesty, might, and authority, from all ages past, and now, and forever and ever! Amen' (vv. 24–25).

The Letter from Jude, while shorter than 2 Peter, covers much of the same ground. While it appears here later in the sequence of our Bible, almost all who have compared the two books do not think that they draw on a common source but that 2 Peter draws on Jude and incorporates much of it into his own letter. If that is the case, in fairness to Jude, his letter should have been discussed first and in greater detail, but that would have been confusing to the readers of this book. Much of the teaching has already been introduced in the chapter on 2 Peter, and now only a few references to special material need be added.

Both books include accounts of God's judgements in the past, though Jude omits reference to the Flood and 2 Peter omits Jude's references to Israelites who disobeyed. Jude does not have his references in the right chronological order, whereas 2 Peter does. This would make it appear that 2 Peter is later, a kind of 'improvement' on the original document. Jude (v. 9) names one of the angels, Michael, while Peter names none. Line by line analyses show reasons why 2 Peter would have made the changes rather than Jude drawing on Peter.

False Teachers

Jude speaks of 'the salvation we share in common' and 'the faith which once and for all God has given to his people' (v. 3) as if these are deposits carefully to be guarded, objects for simple definition. He faces the same problem Peter does; godless teachers have 'slipped in unnoticed among us' ('wormed their way in') (v. 4). They are not named leaders of a faction that was out to confuse and seduce Christians. He refers to the fact that 'long ago the Scriptures predicted this condemnation they have received,' and then includes references both to the Old Testament and probably to 1 Enoch and possibly other non-biblical writings.

The references to fallen angels or to Sodom and

Gomorrah and the like, are familiar from 2 Peter, but
Michael is a fresh name here. He is discussed in a book
called 'The Assumption of Moses'. In it, Moses is dead
and Michael is sent forth to pick up his body. But the
Devil will not permit this since Moses is part of the world
of matter, over which the Devil rules. He could also
accuse Moses of having sinned. Michael has the Lord
condemn the Devil, while he guards Israel. The book of
Daniel sees him as one of the most important angels.

Cain and Korah are added to the earlier reference in
2 Peter to Balaam (or, shall we say, they were dropped
by 2 Peter?). Cain was the first murderer, hardly a
flattering person for comparison to the false teachers.
They are going the way of all murderers. Korah
(Numbers 16:1-35) refused to accept Moses' and Aaron's
authority and was punished. The new false teachers
also reject proper church authority. With a number of
colourful phrases these teachers are dismissed (vv. 12-13).
Enoch, a biblical character referred to in extra-biblical
books on which Jude draws, is introduced as one who
offers or announces judgement on false teachers.

Warnings and Instructions

The final reminders are rather routine, except for verse
18 where we are told in direct quotations of a warning
by the apostles. 'When the last days come, men will
appear who will make fun of you, men who follow their
own godless desires.' It is not possible to find this reference
in the New Testament, but the general idea of opposition
is prophesied again and again. When the believers are
asked to 'pray in the power of the Holy Spirit, and keep
yourselves in the love of God, as you wait for our Lord
Jesus Christ in his mercy to give you eternal life' (v.
20-21), we have an anticipation of the later development
of language referring to three 'persons' of the divine
Trinity. Some of Paul's greetings, as in 2 Corinthians
13:13, reveal a similar completeness.

Prayer of Praise

People who know nothing else about Jude have very likely heard a blessing based on his closing doxology. 'To him who is able to keep you from falling and bring you faultless and joyful before his glorious presence' – the Christian does not bring a sacrificial gift to make himself worthy. His standing before the Lord is a gift. While any number of earthly forces might claim authority, God alone has all glory, majesty, power, and authority. We can picture that the people who first received this greeting, mired as they were in controversy, swept by confusion, fearful of the future, must have thrilled to see that their daily lives were part of a large drama, the drama of the ages, the context and fulfilment of the Good News. The words have the same effect on people who hear them afresh today.

PAUL'S FIRST LETTER TO TIMOTHY

1 From Paul, an apostle of Christ Jesus by order of God our Saviour and Christ Jesus our hope—
²To Timothy, my true son in the faith:
May God the Father and Christ Jesus our Lord give you grace, mercy, and peace.

Warnings against False Teaching

³I want you to stay in Ephesus, just as I urged you when I was on my way to Macedonia. Some people there are teaching false doctrines, and you must order them to stop. ⁴Tell them to give up those legends and those long lists of names of ancestors, because these only produce arguments; they do not serve God's plan, which is known by faith. ⁵The purpose of this order is to arouse the love that comes from a pure heart, a clear conscience, and a genuine faith. ⁶Some men have turned away from these and have lost their way in foolish discussions. ⁷They want to be teachers of God's law, but they do not understand their own words or the matters about which they speak with so much confidence.

⁸We know that the Law is good, if it is used as it should be used. ⁹It must be remembered, of course, that laws are made, not for good people, but for lawbreakers and criminals, for the godless and sinful, for those who are not religious or spiritual, for men who kill their fathers or mothers, for murderers, ¹⁰for the immoral, for sexual perverts, for kidnappers, for those who lie and give false testimony or do anything else contrary to the true teaching. ¹¹That teaching is found in the gospel that was entrusted to me to announce, the Good News from the glorious and blessed God.

Gratitude for God's Mercy

¹²I give thanks to Christ Jesus our Lord, who has given me strength for my work. I thank him for considering me worthy, and appointing me to serve him, ¹³even though in the past I spoke evil of him, and persecuted and insulted him. But God was merciful to me,

because I did not believe and so did not know what I was doing. ¹⁴And our Lord poured out his abundant grace on me and gave me the faith and love which are ours in union with Christ Jesus. ¹⁵This is a true saying, to be completely accepted and believed: Christ Jesus came into the world to save sinners. I am the worst of them, ¹⁶but it was for this very reason that God was merciful to me, in order that Christ Jesus might show his full patience in dealing with me, the worst of sinners, as an example for all those who would later believe in him and receive eternal life. ¹⁷To the eternal King, immortal and invisible, the only God—to him be honour and glory forever and ever! Amen.

Christ Jesus came into the world to save sinners

¹⁸Timothy, my child, I entrust this command to you. It is according to the words of prophecy spoken long ago about you. Let those words be your weapons as you fight the good fight, ¹⁹and keep your faith and clear conscience. Some men have not listened to their conscience, and have made a ruin of their faith. ²⁰Among them are Hymenaeus and Alexander, whom

I have handed over to the power of Satan, so that they will be taught to stop speaking evil of God.

Church Worship

2 First of all, then, I urge that petitions, prayers, requests, and thanksgivings be offered to God for all men; ²for kings and all others who are in authority, that we may live a quiet and peaceful life, in entire godliness and proper conduct. ³This is good and it pleases God our Saviour, ⁴who wants all men to be saved and to come to know the truth. ⁵For there is one God, and there is one who brings God and men together, the man Christ Jesus, ⁶who gave himself to redeem all men. That was the proof, at the right time, that God wants all men to be saved, ⁷and this is why I was sent as an apostle and teacher of the Gentiles, to proclaim the message of faith and truth. I am not lying, I am telling the truth!

⁸I want men everywhere to pray, men who are dedicated to God and can lift up their hands in prayer without anger or argument.

⁹I also want women to be modest and sensible about their clothes and to dress properly; not with fancy hair styles, or with gold ornaments or pearls or expensive dresses, ¹⁰but with good deeds, as is proper for women who claim to be religious. ¹¹Women should learn in silence and all humility. ¹²I do not allow women to teach or to have authority over men; they must keep quiet. ¹³For Adam was created first, and then Eve. ¹⁴And it was not Adam who was deceived; it was the woman who was deceived and broke God's law. ¹⁵But a woman will be saved through having children, if she perseveres in faith and love and holiness, with modesty.

Leaders in the Church

3 This is a true saying: If a man is eager to be a church leader he desires an excellent work. ²A church leader must be a man without fault; he must have only one wife, be sober, self-controlled, and orderly; he must welcome strangers in his home; he must be able to teach; ³he must not be a drunkard or a violent man, but gentle and peaceful; he must not love money; ⁴he must be able to manage his own family well, and make his children obey him with all respect. ⁵For if a man does not know

how to manage his own family, how can he take care of the church of God? 6He must not be a man who has been recently converted; else he will swell up with pride and be condemned, as the Devil was. 7He should be a man who is respected by the people outside the church, so that he will not be disgraced and fall into the Devil's trap.

Helpers in the Church

8Church helpers must also be of a good character and sincere; they must not drink too much wine or be greedy; 9they should hold to the revealed truth of the faith with a clear conscience. 10They should be tested first, and then, if they pass the test, they should serve. 11Their wives also must be of good character, and not gossip; they must be sober and honest in everything. 12A church helper must have only one wife, and be able to manage his children and family well. 13Those who do a good work win for themselves a good standing and are able to speak boldly about their faith in Christ Jesus.

The Great Secret

14As I write this letter to you, I hope to come and see you soon. 15But if I delay, this letter will let you know how we should conduct ourselves in God's household, which is the church of the living God, the pillar and support of the truth. 16No one can deny how great is the secret of our religion.

> He appeared in human form,
>> was shown to be right by the Spirit,
>> and was seen by angels.
> He was preached among the nations,
>> was believed in the world, and was
>> taken up to heaven.

False Teachers

4 The Spirit says clearly that some men will abandon the faith in later times; they will obey lying spirits and follow the teachings of demons. 2These teachings come from the deceit of men who are liars, and whose consciences are dead, as if burnt with a hot iron. 3Such men teach that it is wrong to marry and to eat certain

foods. But God created these foods to be eaten, after a prayer of thanks, by those who are believers and have come to know the truth. ⁴Everything that God has created is good; nothing is to be rejected, but all is to be received with a prayer of thanks; ⁵because the word of God and the prayer make it acceptable to God.

A Good Servant of Christ Jesus

⁶If you give these instructions to the brothers you will be a good servant of Christ Jesus, as you feed yourself spiritually on the words of faith and of the true teaching which you have followed. ⁷But keep away from those godless legends, which are not worth telling. Keep yourself in training for a godly life. ⁸Physical exercise has some value in it, but spiritual exercise is valuable in every way, because it promises life both for now and for the future. ⁹This is a true saying, to be completely accepted and believed. ¹⁰That is why we struggle and work hard, because we have placed our hope in the living God, who is Saviour of all men, and especially of those who believe.

¹¹Command and teach these things. ¹²Do not let anyone look down on you because you are young, but be an example for the believers, in your speech, your conduct, your love, faith, and purity. ¹³Give your time and effort, until I come, to the public reading of the Scriptures, and to preaching and teaching. ¹⁴Do not neglect the spiritual gift that is in you, which was given to you when the prophets spoke and the elders laid their hands on you. ¹⁵Practise these things and give yourself to them, in order that your progress may be seen by all. ¹⁶Watch yourself, and watch your teaching. Keep on doing these things, because if you do you will save both yourself and those who hear you.

Responsibilities towards Believers

5 Do not rebuke an older man, but appeal to him as if he were your father. Treat the younger men as your brothers, ²the older women as mothers, and the younger women as sisters, with all purity.

³Show respect for widows who really are widows. ⁴But if a widow has children or grandchildren, they

should learn first to carry out their religious duties towards their own family and in this way repay their parents and grandparents, because that is what pleases God. [5]The woman who is a true widow, with no one to take care of her, has placed her hope in God and continues to pray and ask him for his help night and day. [6]But the widow who gives herself to pleasure has already died, even though she lives. [7]Give them this command, so that no one will find fault with them. [8]But if someone does not take care of his relatives, especially the members of his own family, he has denied the faith and is worse than an unbeliever.

[9]Do not add any widow to the list of widows unless she is more than sixty years old. In addition, she must have been married only once, [10]and have a reputation for good deeds: a woman who brought up her children well, received strangers in her home, washed the feet of God's people, helped those in trouble, and gave herself to all kinds of good works.

[11]But do not include the younger widows in the list; because when their desires make them want to marry, they turn away from Christ, [12]and so become guilty of breaking their first promise to him. [13]They also learn to waste their time in going round from house to house; but even worse, they learn to be gossips and busybodies, talking of things they should not. [14]So I would rather that the younger widows get married, have children, and take care of their homes, so as to give our enemies no chance of speaking evil of us. [15]For some widows have already turned away to follow Satan. [16]But if any woman who is a believer has widows in her family, she must take care of them, and not put the burden on the church, so that it may take care of the widows who are all alone.

[17]The elders who do good work as leaders should be considered worthy of receiving double pay, especially those who work hard at preaching and teaching. [18]For the scripture says, "Do not tie up the mouth of the ox when it is treading out the grain," and, "The worker deserves his wages." [19]Do not listen to an accusation against an elder unless it is brought by two or three witnesses. [20]Rebuke publicly all those who commit sins, so that the rest may be afraid.

Do not tie up the mouth

²¹In the presence of God, and of Christ Jesus, and of the holy angels, I solemnly call upon you to obey these instructions without showing any prejudice or favour to anyone in anything you do. ²²Be in no hurry to lay hands on anyone for the Lord's service. Take no part in the sins of others; keep yourself pure.

²³Do not drink water only, but take a little wine to help your digestion, since you are sick so often.

²⁴The sins of some men are plain to see, and their sins go ahead of them to judgment; but the sins of others are seen only later. ²⁵In the same way good deeds are plainly seen, and even those that are not so plain cannot be hidden.

6 All who are slaves must consider their masters worthy of all respect, so that no one will speak evil of the name of God and of our teaching. ²Slaves belonging to masters who are believers must not despise them because they are their brothers. Instead, they are to serve them even better, because those who benefit from their work are believers whom they love.

False Teaching and True Riches

You must teach and preach these things. ³Whoever teaches a different doctrine and does not agree with the true words of our Lord Jesus Christ and with the teaching of our religion ⁴is swollen with pride and knows nothing. He has an unhealthy desire to argue and quarrel about words, and this brings on jealousy, dissension, insults, evil suspicions, [5]and constant arguments from men whose minds do not function and who no longer have the truth. They think that religion is a way to become rich.

[6]Well, religion does make a man very rich, if he is satisfied with what he has. [7]What did we bring into the world? Nothing! What can we take out of the world? Nothing! [8]So then, if we have food and clothes, that should be enough for us. [9]But those who want to get rich fall into temptation and are caught in the trap of many foolish and harmful desires, which pull men down to ruin and destruction. [10]For the love of money is a source of all kinds of evil. Some have been so eager to have it that they have wandered away from the faith and have broken their hearts with many sorrows.

Personal Instructions

[11]But you, man of God, avoid all these things. Strive for righteousness, godliness, faith, love, endurance, and gentleness. [12]Run your best in the race of faith, and win eternal life for yourself; for it was to this life that God called you when you made your good profession of faith before many witnesses. [13]Before God, who gives life to all things, and before Christ Jesus, who made the good profession before Pontius Pilate, I command you: [14]Obey the commandment and keep it pure and faultless, until the Day our Lord Jesus Christ will appear. [15]His appearing will be brought about at the right time by God, the blessed and only Ruler, the King of kings and the Lord of lords. [16]He alone is immortal; he lives in the light that no one can approach. No one has ever seen him, no one can ever see him. To him be honour and eternal might! Amen.

[17]Command those who are rich in the things of this life not to be proud, and to place their hope, not in such an uncertain thing as riches, but in God, who generously gives us everything for us to enjoy. [18]Command them to do good, to be rich in good works, to be generous and ready to share with others. [19]In this way they will store up for themselves a treasure which will be a solid foun-

dation for the future. And then they will be able to win the life which is true life.

[20]Timothy, keep safe what has been turned over to your care. Avoid the godless talk and foolish arguments of "Knowledge," as some people wrongly call it. [21]For some have claimed to possess it, and as a result they have lost the way of faith.

God's grace be with you all.

PAUL'S SECOND LETTER TO TIMOTHY

1 From Paul, an apostle of Christ Jesus by God's will, sent to proclaim the promised life which we have in union with Christ Jesus—

[2] To Timothy, my dear son:

May God the Father and Christ Jesus our Lord give you grace, mercy, and peace.

Thanksgiving and Encouragement

[3] I give thanks to God, whom I serve with a clear conscience, as my ancestors did. I thank him as I remember you always in my prayers, night and day. [4] I remember your tears, and I want to see you very much, so that I may be filled with joy. [5] I remember the sincere faith you have, the kind of faith that your grandmother Lois and your mother Eunice also had. I am sure that you have it also. [6] For this reason I remind you to keep alive the gift that God gave to you when I laid my hands on you. [7] For the Spirit that God has given us does not make us timid; instead, his Spirit fills us with power, love, and self-control.

[8] Do not be ashamed, then, of witnessing for our Lord; neither be ashamed of me, his prisoner. Instead, take your part in suffering for the Good News, as God gives you the strength for it. [9] He saved us and called us to be his own people, not because of what we have done, but because of his own purpose and grace. He gave us this grace by means of Christ Jesus before the beginning of time, [10] but now it has been revealed to us through the coming of our Saviour, Christ Jesus. He has ended the power of death, and through the Good News has revealed immortal life.

[11] God has appointed me to proclaim the Good News as an apostle and teacher, [12] and it is for this reason that I suffer these things. But I am still full of confidence, because I know whom I have trusted, and I am sure that he is able to keep safe until that Day what he has entrusted to me. [13] Hold to the true words that I taught you, as the example for you to follow, and stay in the

faith and love that are ours in union with Christ Jesus.
¹⁴Keep the good things that have been entrusted to you,
through the power of the Holy Spirit, who lives in us.

¹⁵You know that everyone in the province of Asia
deserted me, including Phygelus and Hermogenes.
¹⁶May the Lord show mercy to the family of Onesiphorus, because he cheered me up many times. He was
not ashamed that I am in prison, ¹⁷but as soon as he
arrived in Rome he started looking for me until he found
me. ¹⁸May the Lord grant him to receive mercy from the
Lord on that Day! And you know very well how much
he did for me in Ephesus.

A Loyal Soldier of Christ Jesus

2 As for you, my son, be strong through the grace
that is ours in union with Christ Jesus. ²Take the
words that you heard me preach in the presence of many
witnesses, and give them into the keeping of men you
can trust, men who will be able to teach others also.

Take your part in suffering

³Take your part in suffering, as a loyal soldier of
Christ Jesus. ⁴A soldier in active service wants to please
his commanding officer, and so does not get mixed up
in the affairs of civilian life. ⁵An athlete who runs in a
race cannot win the prize unless he obeys the rules. ⁶The
farmer who has done the hard work should have the first
share of the harvest. ⁷Think about what I am saying,
because the Lord will enable you to understand all
things.

⁸Remember Jesus Christ, who was raised from death, who was a descendant of David, as told in the Good News I preach. ⁹Because I preach the Good News I suffer, and I am even chained like a criminal. But the word of God is not in chains, ¹⁰and for this reason I endure everything for the sake of God's chosen people, in order that they too may obtain the salvation that is in Christ Jesus, together with eternal glory. ¹¹This is a true saying:

"If we have died with him,
    we shall also live with him.
¹² If we continue to endure,
    we shall also rule with him.
If we deny him,
    he also will deny us.
¹³ If we are not faithful,
    he remains faithful,
    because he cannot be false to himself."

An Approved Worker

¹⁴Remind your people of this, and give them solemn warning in God's presence not to fight over words. It does no good, but only ruins the people who listen. ¹⁵Do your best to win full approval in God's sight, as a worker who is not ashamed of his work, one who correctly teaches the message of God's truth. ¹⁶Keep away from godless and foolish discussions, which only drive people farther away from God. ¹⁷What they teach will be like an open sore that eats away the flesh. Two of these teachers are Hymenaeus and Philetus. ¹⁸They have left the way of truth and are upsetting the faith of some believers by saying that our resurrection has already taken place. ¹⁹But the solid foundation that God has laid cannot be shaken; and these words are written on it: "The Lord knows those who are his"; and, "Whoever says that he belongs to the Lord must turn away from wrongdoing."

²⁰In a large house there are dishes and bowls of all kinds: some are made of silver and gold, others of wood and clay; some are for special occasions, others for ordinary use. ²¹If anyone makes himself clean from all these

evil things, he will be used for special purposes, because he is dedicated and useful to his Master, ready to be used for every good work. ²²Avoid the passions of youth, and strive for righteousness, faith, love, and peace, together with those who with a pure heart call for the Lord to help them. ²³But stay away from foolish and ignorant arguments; you know that they end up in quarrels. ²⁴The Lord's servant must not quarrel. He must be kind towards all, a good and patient teacher, ²⁵who is gentle as he corrects his opponents. It may be that God will give them the opportunity to repent and come to know the truth. ²⁶And then they will return to their senses and escape from the trap of the Devil, who had caught them and made them obey his will.

The Last Days

3 Remember this! There will be difficult times in the last days. ²Men will be selfish, greedy, boastful, and conceited; they will be insulting, disobedient to their parents, ungrateful, and irreligious; ³they will be unkind, merciless, slanderers, violent, and fierce; they will hate the good; ⁴they will be treacherous, reckless, and swollen with pride; they will love pleasure rather than God; ⁵they will hold to the outward form of our religion, but reject its real power. Keep away from these men. ⁶Some of them go into homes and get control over weak women who are burdened by the guilt of their sins and driven by all kinds of desires, ⁷women who are always trying to learn but who never can come to know the truth. ⁸As Jannes and Jambres were opposed to Moses, so also these men are opposed to the truth—men whose minds do not function and who are failures in the faith. ⁹But they will not get very far, because everyone will see how stupid they are, just as it happened to Jannes and Jambres.

Last Instructions

¹⁰But you have followed my teaching, my conduct, and my purpose in life; you have observed my faith, my

patience, my love, my endurance, [11]my persecutions, and my sufferings. You know all the things that happened to me in Antioch, Iconium, and Lystra, the terrible persecutions I endured! But the Lord rescued me from them all. [12]All who want to live a godly life in union with Christ Jesus will be persecuted; [13]but evil men and impostors will keep on going from bad to worse, deceiving others and being deceived themselves. [14]But as for you, continue in the truths that you were taught and firmly believe. You know who your teachers were, [15]and you remember that ever since you were a child you have known the Holy Scriptures, which are able to give you the wisdom that leads to salvation through faith in Christ Jesus. [16]All Scripture is inspired by God and is useful for teaching the truth, rebuking error, correcting faults, and giving instruction for right living, [17]so that the man who serves God may be fully qualified and equipped to do every kind of good work.

4 I solemnly urge you in the presence of God and of Christ Jesus, who will judge all men, living and dead: because of his coming and of his Kingdom, I command you [2]to preach the message, to insist upon telling it, whether the time is right or not; to convince, reproach, and encourage, teaching with all patience. [3]The time will come when men will not listen to the true teaching, but will follow their own desires, and will collect for themselves more and more teachers who will tell them what they are itching to hear. [4]They will turn away from listening to the truth and give their attention to legends. [5]But you must keep control of yourself in all circumstances; endure suffering, do the work of a preacher of the Good News, and perform your whole duty as a servant of God.

[6]As for me, the hour has come for me to be sacrificed; the time is here for me to leave this life. [7]I have done my best in the race, I have run the full distance, I have kept the faith. [8]And now the prize of victory is waiting for me, the crown of righteousness which the Lord, the righteous Judge, will give me on that Day—and not only to me, but to all those who wait with love for him to appear.

The prize of victory is waiting for me

Personal Words

⁹Do your best to come to me soon. ¹⁰Demas fell in love with this present world and has deserted me; he has gone off to Thessalonica. Crescens went to Galatia, and Titus to Dalmatia. ¹¹Only Luke is with me. Get Mark and bring him with you, because he can help me in the work. ¹²I sent Tychicus to Ephesus. ¹³When you come, bring my coat that I left in Troas with Carpus; bring the books too, and especially the ones made of parchment.

¹⁴Alexander the metalworker did me great harm; the Lord will reward him according to what he has done. ¹⁵Be on your guard against him yourself, because he was violently opposed to our message.

¹⁶No one stood by me the first time I defended myself; all deserted me. May God not count it against them! ¹⁷But the Lord stayed with me and gave me strength, so that I was able to proclaim the full message for all the Gentiles to hear; and I was rescued from the lion's mouth. ¹⁸And the Lord will rescue me from all evil, and take me safely into his heavenly Kingdom. To him be the glory forever and ever! Amen.

Final Greetings

[19]I send greetings to Priscilla and Aquila, and to the family of Onesiphorus. [20]Erastus stayed in Corinth, and I left Trophimus in Miletus, because he was sick. [21]Do your best to come before winter.

Eubulus, Pudens, Linus, and Claudia send their greetings, and so do all the other brothers.

[22]The Lord be with your spirit.

God's grace be with you all.

PAUL'S LETTER TO TITUS

1 From Paul, a servant of God and an apostle of Jesus Christ.

I was chosen and sent to help the faith of God's chosen people and lead them to the truth taught by our religion, [2]which is based on the hope for eternal life. God, who does not lie, promised us this life before the beginning of time, [3]and at the right time he revealed it in his message. This was entrusted to me, and I proclaim it by order of God our Saviour.

[4]I write to Titus, my true son in the faith that we share:

May God the Father and Christ Jesus our Saviour give you grace and peace.

Titus' Work in Crete

[5]I left you in Crete for you to put in order the things that still needed doing, and to appoint church elders in every town. Remember my instructions: [6]an elder must be without fault; he must have only one wife, and his children must be believers and not have the reputation of being wild or disobedient. [7]For since he is in charge of God's work, the church leader should be without fault. He must not be arrogant or quick-tempered, or a drunkard, or violent, or greedy. [8]He must be hospitable and love what is good. He must be self-controlled, upright, holy, and disciplined. [9]He must hold firmly to the message which can be trusted and which agrees with the doctrine. In this way he will be able to encourage others with the true teaching, and also show the error of those who are opposed to it.

[10]For there are many who rebel and deceive others with their nonsense, especially the converts from Judaism. [11]It is necessary to stop their talking, because they are upsetting whole families by teaching what they should not, for the shameful purpose of making money. [12]It was a Cretan himself, one of their own prophets, who said, "Cretans are always liars, wicked beasts, and lazy gluttons." [13]And what he said is true. For this reason you must rebuke them sharply, so that they may

have a healthy faith, [14]and no longer hold on to Jewish legends and to human commandments which come from men who have rejected the truth. [15]Everything is pure to those who are themselves pure; but nothing is pure to those who are defiled and unbelieving, because their minds and consciences have been defiled. [16]They claim that they know God, but their actions deny it. They are hateful and disobedient, not fit to do anything good.

Sound Doctrine

2 But you must teach what is required by sound doctrine. [2]Tell the older men to be sober, sensible, and self-controlled; to be sound in their faith, love, and endurance. [3]In the same way tell the older women to behave as women who live a holy life should. They must not be slanderers, or slaves to wine. They must teach what is good, [4]in order to train the younger women to love their husbands and children, [5]to be self-controlled and pure, and to be good housewives, who obey their husbands, so that no one will speak evil of the message from God.

[6]In the same way urge the young men to be self-controlled. [7]You yourself, in all things, must be an example in good works. Be sincere and serious in your teaching. [8]Use sound words that cannot be criticized, so that your enemies may be put to shame by not having anything bad to say about us.

[9]Slaves are to obey their masters and please them in all things. They must not talk back to them, [10]or steal from them. Instead, they must show that they are always good and faithful, so as to bring credit to the teaching about God our Saviour in all they do.

[11]For God has revealed his grace for the salvation of all men. [12]That grace instructs us to give up ungodly living and worldly passions, and to live self-controlled, upright, and godly lives in this world, [13]as we wait for the blessed Day we hope for, when the glory of our great God and Saviour Jesus Christ will appear. [14]He gave himself for us, to rescue us from all wickedness and make us a pure people who belong to him alone and are eager to do good.

¹⁵Teach these things, and use your full authority as you encourage and rebuke your hearers. Let none of them look down on you.

Christian Conduct

3 Remind your people to submit to rulers and authorities, to obey them, to be ready to do every good thing. ²Tell them not to speak evil of anyone, but to be peaceful and friendly, and always show a gentle attitude towards all men. ³For we ourselves were once foolish, disobedient, and wrong. We were slaves to passions and pleasures of all kinds. We spent our lives in malice and envy; others hated us and we hated them. ⁴But when the kindness and love of God our Saviour appeared, ⁵he saved us. It was not because of any good works that we ourselves had done, but because of his own mercy that he saved us through the washing by which the Holy Spirit gives us new birth and new life. ⁶God poured out the Holy Spirit abundantly on us, through Jesus Christ our Saviour, ⁷so that by his grace we might be put right with God and come into possession of the eternal life we hope for. ⁸This is a true saying.

I want you to give special emphasis to these matters, so that those who believe in God may be concerned with giving their time to doing good works. These are good and useful for men. ⁹But avoid stupid arguments, long lists of names of ancestors, quarrels, and fights about the Law. They are useless and worthless. ¹⁰Give at least two warnings to the man who causes divisions, and then have nothing more to do with him. ¹¹You know that such a person is corrupt, and his sins prove that he is wrong.

Final Instructions

¹²When I send Artemas or Tychicus to you, do your best to come to me in Nicopolis, because I have decided to spend the winter there. ¹³Do your best to help Zenas the lawyer and Apollos to get started on their travels, and see to it that they have everything they need. ⁴Have our people learn to give their time in doing good

works, to provide for real needs; they should not live useless lives.

[15]All who are with me send you greetings. Give our greetings to our friends in the faith.

God's grace be with you all.

THE LETTER FROM JAMES

1 From James, a servant of God and of the Lord Jesus Christ:

Greetings to all God's people, scattered over the whole world.

Faith and Wisdom

²My brothers! Consider yourselves fortunate when all kinds of trials come your way, ³because you know that when your faith succeeds in facing such trials, the result is the ability to endure. ⁴Be sure that your endurance carries you all the way, without failing, so that you may be perfect and complete, lacking nothing. ⁵But if any of you lacks wisdom, he should pray to God, who will give it to him; because God gives generously and graciously to all. ⁶But you must believe when you pray, and not doubt at all. Whoever doubts is like a wave in the sea that is driven and blown about by the wind. ⁷⁻⁸Such a person is a hypocrite, undecided in all he does, and he must not think that he will receive anything from the Lord.

Poverty and Riches

⁹The poor brother must be glad when God lifts him up, ¹⁰and the rich brother when God brings him down. For the rich will pass away like the bloom of a wild plant. ¹¹The sun rises with its blazing heat and burns the plant; its bloom falls off, and its beauty is destroyed. In the same way the rich man will be destroyed while busy conducting his affairs.

Testing and Tempting

¹²Happy is the man who remains faithful under trials, because when he succeeds in passing the test he will receive as his reward the life which God has promised to those who love him. ¹³If a man is tempted by such testing, he must not say, "This temptation comes from God." For God cannot be tempted by evil, and he himself tempts no one. ¹⁴But a person is tempted when he is drawn away and trapped by his own evil desire.

¹⁵Then his evil desire conceives and gives birth to sin; and sin, when it is full-grown, gives birth to death.

¹⁶Do not be deceived, my dear brothers! ¹⁷Every good gift and every perfect present comes from heaven; it comes down from God, the Creator of the heavenly lights. He himself does not change or cause darkness by turning. ¹⁸By his own will he brought us into being through the word of truth, so that we should have first place among all his creatures.

Hearing and Doing

¹⁹Remember this, my dear brothers! Everyone must be quick to listen, but slow to speak, and slow to become angry. ²⁰Man's anger does not achieve God's righteous purpose. ²¹Rid yourselves, then, of every filthy habit and all wicked conduct. Submit to God and accept the word that he plants in your hearts, which is able to save you.

²²Do not fool yourselves by just listening to his word. Instead, put it into practice. ²³Whoever listens to the word but does not put it into practice is like a man who looks in a mirror and sees himself as he is. ²⁴He takes a good look at himself and then goes away, and at once forgets what he looks like. ²⁵But whoever looks closely into the perfect law that sets men free, who keeps on paying attention to it, and does not simply listen and

Take care of orphans and widows

then forget it, but puts it into practice—that person will be blessed by God in what he does.

²⁶Does anyone think he is a religious man? If he does not control his tongue his religion is worthless and he deceives himself. ²⁷What God the Father considers to be pure and genuine religion is this: to take care of orphans and widows in their suffering, and to keep oneself from being corrupted by the world.

Warning against Prejudice

2 My brothers! As believers in our Lord Jesus Christ, the Lord of glory, you must never treat people in different ways, according to their outward appearance. ²Suppose a rich man wearing a gold ring and fine clothes comes to your meeting, and a poor man in ragged clothes also comes. ³If you show more respect to the well-dressed man and say to him, "Have this best seat here," but say to the poor man, "Stand, or sit down here on the floor by my feet," ⁴then you are guilty of creating distinctions among yourselves and of making judgments based on evil motives.

God chose the poor

⁵Listen, my dear brothers! God chose the poor people of this world to be rich in faith and to possess the Kingdom which he promised to those who love him. ⁶But you dishonour the poor! Who are the ones who oppress you and drag you before the judges? The rich!

⁷They are the ones who speak evil of that good name which has been given to you.

⁸You will be doing the right thing if you obey the law of the Kingdom, which is found in the scripture, "Love your fellow-man as yourself." ⁹But if you treat people according to their outward appearance, you are guilty of sin, and the Law condemns you as a law-breaker. ¹⁰Whoever breaks one command of the Law is guilty of breaking them all. ¹¹For the same one who said, "Do not commit adultery," also said, "Do not murder." Even if you do not commit adultery, you have become a lawbreaker if you murder. ¹²Speak and act as people who will be judged by the law that sets men free. ¹³For God will not show mercy when he judges the man who has not been merciful; but mercy triumphs over judgment.

Faith and Actions

¹⁴My brothers! What good is it for someone to say, "I have faith," if his actions do not prove it? Can that faith save him? ¹⁵Suppose there are brothers or sisters who need clothes and don't have enough to eat. ¹⁶What good is there in your saying to them, "God bless you! Keep warm and eat well!"—if you don't give them the necessities of life? ¹⁷So it is with faith: if it is alone and has no actions with it, then it is dead.

¹⁸But someone will say, "One person has faith, another has actions." My answer is, "Show me how anyone can have faith without actions. I will show you my faith by my actions." ¹⁹Do you believe that there is only one God? Good! The demons also believe—and tremble with fear. ²⁰You fool! Do you want to be shown that faith without actions is useless? ²¹How was our ancestor Abraham put right with God? It was through his actions, when he offered his son Isaac on the altar. ²²Can't you see? His faith and his actions worked together; his faith was made perfect through his actions. ²³And the scripture came true that said, "Abraham believed God, and because of his faith God accepted him as righteous." And so Abraham was called God's friend. ²⁴You see, then, that a man is put right with God by what he does, and not because of his faith alone.

²⁵It was the same with the prostitute Rahab. She was put right with God through her actions, by welcoming the Jewish messengers and helping them escape by a different road.

²⁶So then, as the body without the spirit is dead, also faith without actions is dead.

The Tongue

3 My brothers! Not many of you should become teachers, because you know that we teachers will be judged with greater strictness than others. ²All of us often make mistakes. The person who never makes a mistake in what he says is perfect, able also to control his whole being. ³We put a bit into the mouth of a horse to make it obey us, and we are able to make it go where we want. ⁴Or think of a ship: big as it is, and driven by such strong winds, it can be steered by a very small rudder, and goes wherever the pilot wants it to go. ⁵So it is with the tongue: small as it is, it can boast about great things.

Man is able to tame

Just think how large a forest can be set on fire by a tiny flame! ⁶And the tongue is like a fire. It is a world of wrong, occupying its place in our bodies and spreading evil through our whole being. It sets on fire the entire course of our existence with the fire that comes to it from hell itself. ⁷Man is able to tame, and has tamed, all other creatures—wild animals and birds, reptiles and fish. ⁸But no man has ever been able to tame the tongue. It is evil and uncontrollable, full of deadly poison. ⁹We use it to give thanks to our Lord and Father, and also

to curse our fellow-men, created in the likeness of God.
[10]Words of thanksgiving and cursing pour out from the
same mouth. My brothers! This should not happen!
[11]No spring of water pours out sweet and bitter water
from the same opening. [12]A fig tree, my brothers, cannot
bear olives; a grapevine cannot bear figs; nor can salty
water produce fresh water.

The Wisdom from Above

[13]Is there someone among you who is wise and understanding? He is to prove it by his good life, by his good
deeds performed with humility and wisdom. [14]But if in
your heart you are jealous, bitter, and selfish, then you
must not be proud and tell lies against the truth. [15]This
kind of wisdom does not come down from heaven; it
belongs to the world, it is unspiritual and demonic.
[16]Where there is jealousy and selfishness, there is also
disorder and every kind of evil. [17]But the wisdom from
above is pure, first of all; it is also peaceful, gentle, and
friendly; it is full of compassion and produces a harvest
of good deeds; it is free from prejudice and hypocrisy.
[18]And goodness is the harvest that is produced from the
seeds the peacemakers plant in peace.

Friendship with the World

4 Where do all the fights and quarrels among you
come from? They come from your desires for pleasure, which are constantly fighting within your bodies.
[2]You want things, but you cannot have them, so you are
ready to kill; you strongly desire things, but you cannot
get them, so you quarrel and fight. You do not have what
you want because you do not ask God for it. [3]And when
you ask you do not receive it, because your motives are
bad; you ask for things to use for your own pleasures.
[4]Unfaithful people! Don't you know that to be the
world's friend means to be God's enemy? Whoever
wants to be the world's friend makes himself God's
enemy. [5]Do not think that the scripture means nothing
that says, "The spirit that God placed in us is filled with
fierce desires." [6]But the grace that God gives is even
stronger. As the scripture says, "God resists the proud,
but gives grace to the humble."

[7]So then, submit yourselves to God. Resist the Devil, and he will run away from you. [8]Come near to God, and he will come near to you. Wash your hands, you sinners! Cleanse your hearts, you hypocrites! [9]Be sorrowful, cry, and weep; change your laughter into crying, your joy into gloom! [10]Humble yourselves before the Lord, and he will lift you up.

Warning against Judging a Brother

[11]Do not criticize one another, my brothers. Whoever criticizes his brother, or judges him, criticizes the Law and judges it. If you judge the Law, then you are no longer one who obeys the Law, but one who judges it. [12]God is the only lawgiver and judge. He alone can save and destroy. Who do you think you are, to judge your fellow-man?

Warning against Boasting

[13]Now listen to me, you that say, "Today or tomorrow we will travel to a certain city, where we will stay a year, and go into business and make a lot of money." [14]You don't even know what your life tomorrow will be! You are like a thin fog, which appears for a moment and then disappears. [15]What you should say is this, "If the Lord is willing, we will live and do this or that." [16]But now you are proud, and you boast; all such boasting is wrong.

[17]So then, the person who does not do the good he knows he should do is guilty of sin.

Warning to the Rich

5 And now, you rich people, listen to me! Weep and wail over the miseries that are coming upon you! [2]Your riches have rotted away, and your clothes have been eaten by moths. [3]Your gold and silver are covered with rust, and this rust will be a witness against you, and eat up your flesh like fire. You have piled up riches in these last days. [4]You have not paid the wages to the men who work in your fields. Hear their complaints! The cries of those who gather in your crops have reached the ears of God, the Lord Almighty. [5]Your life here on earth has been full of luxury and pleasure. You have made

yourselves fat for the day of slaughter. ⁶You have condemned and murdered the innocent man, and he does
not resist you.

Patience and Prayer

⁷Be patient, then, my brothers, until the Lord comes.
See how the farmer is patient as he waits for his land to
produce precious crops. He waits patiently for the autumn and spring rains. ⁸You also must be patient. Keep
your hopes high, for the day of the Lord's coming is
near.

⁹Do not complain against one another, my brothers,
so that God will not judge you. The Judge is near, ready
to come in. ¹⁰My brothers, remember the prophets who
spoke in the name of the Lord. Take them as examples
of patient endurance under suffering. ¹¹We call them
happy because they endured. You have heard of Job's
patience, and you know how the Lord provided for him
in the end. For the Lord is full of mercy and compassion.

¹²Above all, my brothers, do not use an oath when
you make a promise; do not swear by heaven, or by
earth, or by anything else. Say only "Yes" when you
mean yes, and "No" when you mean no, so that you will
not come under God's judgment.

This prayer, made in faith, will heal the sick man

¹³Is anyone among you in trouble? He should pray. Is anyone happy? He should sing praises. ¹⁴Is there anyone who is sick? He should call the church elders, who will pray for him and rub oil on him in the name of the Lord. ¹⁵This prayer, made in faith, will heal the sick man; the Lord will restore him to health, and the sins he has committed will be forgiven. ¹⁶So then, confess your sins to one another, and pray for one another, so that you will be healed. The prayer of a good man has a powerful effect. ¹⁷Elijah was the same kind of person that we are. He prayed earnestly that there would be no rain, and no rain fell on the land for three and a half years. ¹⁸Once again he prayed, and the sky poured out its rain and the earth produced its crops.

¹⁹My brothers! If one of you wanders away from the truth, and another one brings him back again, ²⁰remember this: whoever turns a sinner back from his wrong way will save that sinner's soul from death, and bring about the forgiveness of many sins.

THE FIRST LETTER FROM PETER

1 From Peter, apostle of Jesus Christ—
To God's chosen people who live as refugees scattered throughout the provinces of Pontus, Galatia, Cappadocia, Asia, and Bithynia. [2]You were chosen according to the purpose of God the Father, and were made a holy people by his Spirit, to obey Jesus Christ and be cleansed by his blood.

May grace and peace be yours in full measure.

A Living Hope

[3]Let us give thanks to the God and Father of our Lord Jesus Christ! Because of his great mercy, he gave us new life by raising Jesus Christ from the dead. This fills us with a living hope, [4]and so we look forward to possess the rich blessings that God keeps for his people. He keeps them for you in heaven, where they cannot decay or spoil or fade away. [5]They are for you, who through faith are kept safe by God's power for the salvation which is ready to be revealed at the end of time.

[6]Be glad about this, even though it may now be necessary for you to be sad for a while because of the many kinds of trials you suffer. [7]Their purpose is to prove that your faith is genuine. Even gold, which can be destroyed, is tested by fire; and so your faith, which is much more precious than gold, must also be tested, that it may endure. Then you will receive praise and glory and honour on the Day when Jesus Christ is revealed. [8]You love him, although you have not seen him. You believe in him, although you do not now see him. And so you rejoice with a great and glorious joy, which words cannot express, [9]because you are receiving the purpose of your faith, the salvation of your souls.

[10]It was concerning this salvation that the prophets made careful search and investigation; and they prophesied about this gift that God would give you. [11]They tried to find out when the time would be and how it would come. This was the time to which Christ's Spirit in them pointed as the Spirit predicted the sufferings that Christ would have to endure and the glory that

would follow. ¹²God revealed to these prophets that their work was not for their own good, but for yours, as they spoke about those things which you have now heard from the messengers of the Good News, who announced them by the power of the Holy Spirit sent from heaven. These are things which even the angels would like to understand.

A Call to Holy Living

¹³So then, have your minds ready for action. Keep alert, and set your hope completely on the blessing which will be given you when Jesus Christ is revealed. ¹⁴Be obedient to God, and do not allow your lives to be shaped by those desires you had when you were still ignorant. ¹⁵Instead, be holy in all that you do, just as God who called you is holy. ¹⁶The scripture says, "You must be holy, because I am holy."

¹⁷You call him Father, when you pray to God, who judges all men by the same standard, according to what each one has done; so then, spend the rest of your lives here on earth in reverence for him. ¹⁸For you know what was paid to set you free from the worthless manner of life you received from your ancestors. It was not something that loses its value, such as silver or gold; ¹⁹you were set free by the costly sacrifice of Christ, who was like a lamb without defect or spot. ²⁰He had been chosen by God before the creation of the world, and was revealed in these last days for your sake. ²¹Through him you believe in God, who raised him from death and gave him glory; and so your faith and hope are fixed on God.

²²Now that by your obedience to the truth you have purified yourselves and have come to have a sincere love for your fellow believers, love one another earnestly with all your hearts. ²³For through the living and eternal word of God you have been born again as the children of a parent who is immortal, not mortal. ²⁴As the scripture says,

"All men are like the wild grass,
     and all their glory is like its flower.
The grass dies, and its flower falls off,
²⁵   but the word of the Lord remains
          forever."
This is the word that the Good News brought to you.

The Living Stone and the Holy Nation

2 Rid yourselves, therefore, of all evil; no more lying, or hypocrisy, or jealousy, or insulting language. ²Be like newborn babies, always thirsty for the pure spiritual milk, so that by drinking it you may grow up and be saved. ³As the scripture says, "You have tasted the Lord's kindness."

⁴Come to the Lord, the living stone rejected as worthless by men, but chosen as valuable by God. ⁵Come as living stones, and let yourselves be used in building the spiritual temple, where you will serve as holy priests to offer spiritual and acceptable sacrifices to God through Jesus Christ. ⁶For the scripture says,

"I chose a valuable stone,
     which now I place for the cornerstone
          in Zion;
     and whoever believes in him will never
          be disappointed."

⁷This stone is of great value for you that believe; but for those who do not believe:

"The very stone which the builders rejected
     turned out to be the most important
          stone."

⁸And another scripture says,

"This is the stone that will make people
     stumble,
     the rock that will make them fall."

They stumbled because they did not believe in the word; such was God's will for them.

⁹But you are the chosen race, the King's priests, the holy nation, God's own people, chosen to proclaim the wonderful acts of God, who called you from the darkness into his own marvellous light. ¹⁰At one time you were not God's people, but now you are his people; at one time you did not know God's mercy, but now you have received his mercy.

Slaves of God

¹¹I appeal to you, my friends, as strangers and refugees in this world! Do not give in to bodily passions, which are always at war against the soul. ¹²Your con-

duct among the heathen should be so good that when they accuse you of being evildoers they will have to recognize your good deeds, and so praise God on the Day of his coming.

13Submit yourselves, for the Lord's sake, to every human authority: to the Emperor, who is the supreme authority, 14and to the governors, who have been sent by him to punish the evildoers and praise those who do good. 15For God's will is this: he wants you to silence the ignorant talk of foolish men by the good things you do. 16Live as free men; do not use your freedom, however, to cover up any evil, but live as God's slaves. 17Respect all men, love your fellow believers, fear God, and respect the Emperor.

The Example of Christ's Suffering

18You servants must submit yourselves to your masters and show them complete respect, not only to those who are kind and considerate, but also to those who are harsh. 19God will bless you for this, if you endure the pain of undeserved suffering because you are conscious of his will. 20For what credit is there if you endure the beatings you deserve for having done wrong? But if you endure suffering even when you have done right, God will bless you for it. 21It was to this that God called you; because Christ himself suffered for you and left you an example, so that you would follow in his steps. 22He committed no sin; no one ever heard a lie come from his lips. 23When he was insulted he did not answer back with an insult; when he suffered he did not threaten, but placed his hopes in God, the righteous Judge. 24Christ himself carried our sins in his body to the cross, so that we might die to sin and live for righteousness. By his wounds you have been healed. 25You were like sheep that had lost their way; but now you have been brought back to follow the Shepherd and Keeper of your souls.

Wives and Husbands

3   In the same way you wives must submit yourselves to your husbands, so that if some of them do not believe God's word, they will be won over to believe by

your conduct. It will not be necessary for you to say a word, [2] because they will see how pure and reverent your conduct is. [3] You should not use outward aids to make yourselves beautiful, such as the way you fix your hair, or the jewellery you put on, or the dresses you wear. [4] Instead, your beauty should consist of your true inner self, the ageless beauty of a gentle and quiet spirit, which is of the greatest value in God's sight. [5] For the devout women of the past, who hoped in God, used to make themselves beautiful in this way, by submitting themselves to their husbands. [6] Sarah was like that; she obeyed Abraham and called him "My master." You are now her daughters if you do good and are not afraid of anything.

[7] You husbands, also, in living with your wives you must recognize that they are the weaker sex. So you must treat them with respect, because they also will receive, together with you, God's gift of life. Do this so that nothing will interfere with your prayers.

Pay back with a blessing

Suffering for Doing Right

[8] To conclude: you must all have the same thoughts and the same feelings; love one another as brothers, and be kind and humble with one another. [9] Do not pay back evil with evil, or cursing with cursing; instead pay back with a blessing, because a blessing is what God promised to give you when he called you. [10] As the scripture says,

"Whoever wants to enjoy life
and wishes to see good times,

must keep from speaking evil
and stop telling lies.
[11] He must turn away from evil and do good;
he must seek peace and pursue it.
[12] For the Lord keeps his eyes on the righteous
and always listens to their prayers;
but he turns against those who do evil."

[13] Who will harm you if you are eager to do what is good? [14] But even if you should suffer for doing what is right, how happy you are! Do not be afraid of men, and do not worry. [15] But have reverence for Christ in your hearts, and make him your Lord. Be ready at all times to answer anyone who asks you to explain the hope you have in you. [16] But do it with gentleness and respect. Keep your conscience clear, so that when you are insulted, those who speak evil of your good conduct as followers of Christ will be made ashamed of what they say. [17] Because it is better to suffer for doing good, if this should be God's will, than for doing wrong. [18] For Christ himself died for you; once and for all he died for sins, a good man for bad men, in order to lead you to God. He was put to death physically, but made alive spiritually, [19] and in his spiritual existence he went and preached to the imprisoned spirits. [20] These were the spirits of those who had not obeyed God, when he waited patiently during the days that Noah was building the ark. The few people in the ark—eight in all—were saved by the water, [21] which was a figure pointing to baptism, which now saves you. It is not the washing off of bodily dirt, but the promise made to God from a good conscience. It saves you through the resurrection of Jesus Christ, [22] who has gone to heaven and is at the right side of God, ruling over all angels and heavenly authorities and powers.

Changed Lives

4 Since Christ suffered physically, you too must strengthen yourselves with the same way of thinking; because whoever suffers physically is no longer involved with sin. [2] From now on, then, you must live the

rest of your earthly lives controlled by God's will, not by human desires. ³You have spent enough time in the past doing what the heathen like to do. Your lives were spent in indecency, lust, drunkenness, orgies, drinking parties, and the disgusting worship of idols. ⁴And now the heathen are surprised when you do not join them in the same wild and reckless living, and so they insult you. ⁵But they will give an account of themselves to God, who is ready to judge the living and the dead. ⁶That is why the Good News was preached also to the dead, to those who had been judged in their physical existence as all men are judged; it was preached to them so that in their spiritual existence they may live as God lives.

Good Managers of God's Gifts

⁷The end of all things is near. You must be self-controlled and alert, to be able to pray. ⁸Above everything, love one another earnestly, because love covers over many sins. ⁹Open your homes to each other, without complaining. ¹⁰Each one, as a good manager of God's different gifts, must use for the good of others the special gift he has received from God. ¹¹Whoever preaches, must preach God's words; whoever serves, must serve with the strength that God gives him, so that in all things praise may be given to God through Jesus Christ, to whom belong glory and power forever and ever. Amen.

Suffering as a Christian

¹²My dear friends, do not be surprised at the painful test you are suffering, as though something unusual were happening to you. ¹³Rather be glad that you are sharing Christ's sufferings, so that you may be full of joy when his glory is revealed. ¹⁴Happy are you if you are insulted because you are Christ's followers; this means that the glorious Spirit, the Spirit of God, is resting on you. ¹⁵None of you should suffer because he is a murderer, or a thief, or a criminal, or tries to manage other people's business. ¹⁶But if you suffer because you are a Christian, don't be ashamed of it, but thank God that you bear Christ's name.

¹⁷The time has come for the judgment to begin, and God's own people are the first to be judged. If it starts with us, how will it end with those who do not believe the Good News from God? ¹⁸As the scripture says,

"It is difficult for good men to be saved;
　what, then, will become of the godless
　　and sinful?"

¹⁹So then, those who suffer because it is God's will for them, should by their good actions trust themselves completely to their Creator, who always keeps his promise.

The Flock of God

5　I appeal to the church elders among you, I who am an elder myself. I am a witness of Christ's sufferings, and I will share in the glory that will be revealed. I appeal to you: ²be shepherds of the flock that God gave you, and look after it willingly, as God wants you to, and not unwillingly. Do your work, not for mere pay, but from a real desire to serve. ³Do not try to rule over those who have been given into your care, but be examples to the flock. ⁴And when the Chief Shepherd appears, you will receive the glorious crown which will never lose its brightness.

⁵In the same way, you younger men must submit yourselves to the older men. And all of you must put on the apron of humility, to serve one another; for the scripture says, "God resists the proud, but gives grace to the humble." ⁶Humble yourselves, then, under God's mighty hand, so that he will lift you up in his own good time. ⁷Throw all your worries on him, because he cares for you.

⁸Be alert, be on watch! Your enemy, the Devil, roams around like a roaring lion, looking for someone to devour. ⁹Be firm in your faith and resist him, because you know that your fellow believers in all the world are going through the same kind of sufferings. ¹⁰But after you have suffered for a little while, the God of all grace, who calls you to share his eternal glory in union with Christ, will himself perfect you, and give you firmness, strength, and a sure foundation. ¹¹To him be the power forever! Amen.

Final Greetings

¹²I write you this brief letter with the help of Silas, whom I regard as a faithful brother. I want to encourage you and give my testimony that this is the true grace of God. Stand firm in it.

¹³Your sister church in Babylon, also chosen by God, sends you greetings, and so does my son Mark. ¹⁴Greet each other with the kiss of Christian love.

May peace be with all of you who belong to Christ.

The kiss of Christian love

THE SECOND LETTER FROM PETER

1 From Simon Peter, a servant and apostle of Jesus Christ—

To those who through the righteousness of our God and Saviour Jesus Christ have been given a faith as precious as ours:

[2]May grace and peace be yours in full measure, through your knowledge of God and of Jesus our Lord.

God's Call and Choice

[3]God's divine power has given us everything we need to live a godly life through our knowledge of the one who called us to share his own glory and goodness. [4]In this way he has given us the very great and precious gifts he promised, so that by means of these gifts you may escape from the destructive lust that is in the world, and come to share the divine nature. [5]For this very reason do your best to add goodness to your faith; to your goodness add knowledge; [6]to your knowledge add self-control; to your self-control add endurance; to your endurance add godliness; [7]to your godliness add brotherly love; and to your brotherly love add love. [8]These are the qualities you need, and if you have them in abundance they will make you active and effective in your knowledge of our Lord Jesus Christ. [9]But whoever does not have them is so shortsighted that he cannot see, and has forgotten that his past sins have been washed away.

[10]So then, my brothers, try even harder to make God's call and his choice of you a permanent experience; if you do so, you will never fall away. [11]In this way you will be given the full right to enter the eternal Kingdom of our Lord and Saviour Jesus Christ.

[12]For this reason I will always remind you of these matters, even though you already know them and are firmly fixed in the truth you have received. [13]I think it only right for me to stir up your memory of these matters, as long as I am still alive. [14]I know that I shall soon put off this mortal body, as our Lord Jesus Christ plainly told me. [15]I will do my best, then, to provide a way for

you to remember these matters at all times after my death.

Eyewitnesses of Christ's Glory

[16]We have not depended on made-up legends in making known to you the mighty coming of our Lord Jesus Christ. With our own eyes we saw his greatness. [17]We were there when he was given honour and glory by God the Father, when the voice came to him from the Supreme Glory, saying, "This is my own dear Son, with whom I am well pleased!" [18]We ourselves heard this voice coming from heaven, when we were with him on the sacred mountain.

[19]So we are even more confident of the message proclaimed by the prophets. You will do well to pay attention to it, because it is like a lamp shining in a dark place, until the Day dawns and the light of the morning star shines in your hearts. [20]Above all else, however, remember this: no one can explain, by himself, a prophecy in the Scriptures. [21]For no prophetic message ever came just from the will of man, but men were carried along by the Holy Spirit as they spoke the message that came from God.

False Teachers

2 False prophets appeared in the past among the people, and in the same way false teachers will appear among you. They will bring in destructive, untrue doctrines, and deny the Master who redeemed them, and so bring upon themselves sudden destruction. [2]Even so, many will follow their immoral ways; and, because of what they do, people will speak evil of the Way of truth. [3]In their greed these false teachers will make a profit out of telling you made-up stories. For a long time now their Judge has been ready, and their Destroyer has been wide awake!

[4]God did not spare the angels who sinned, but threw them into hell, where they are kept chained in darkness, waiting for the Day of Judgment. [5]God did not spare the ancient world, but brought the Flood on the world of godless men; the only ones he saved were Noah, who preached righteousness, and seven other people. [6]God

condemned the cities of Sodom and Gomorrah, destroying them with fire, and made them an example of what will happen to the godless. [7]He rescued Lot, a good man, who was troubled by the immoral conduct of lawless men. [8]That good man lived among them and day after day saw and heard such things that his good heart was tormented by their evil actions. [9]And so the Lord knows how to rescue godly men from their trials, and how to keep the wicked under punishment for the Day of Judgment, [10]especially those who follow their filthy bodily lusts and despise God's authority.

These false teachers are bold and arrogant, and show no respect for the glorious beings above; instead, they insult them. [11]Even the angels, who are so much stronger and mightier than these false teachers, do not accuse them with insults in the presence of the Lord. [12]But these men act by instinct, like wild animals born to be captured and killed; they insult things they do not understand. They will be destroyed like wild animals; [13]they will be paid with suffering for the suffering they caused. Pleasure for them is to do anything in broad daylight that will satisfy their bodily appetites; they are a shame and a disgrace as they join you in your meals, all the while enjoying their deceitful ways! [14]They want to look at nothing else but immoral women; their appetite for sin is never satisfied. They lead weak people into a trap. Their hearts are trained to be greedy. They are under God's curse! [15]They have left the straight path and have lost their way; they have followed the path taken by Balaam the son of Bosor, who loved the money he would get for doing wrong, [16]and was rebuked for his sin. A dumb ass spoke with a human voice and stopped the prophet's insane action.

[17]These men are like dried-up springs, like clouds blown along by a storm; God has reserved a place for them in the deepest darkness. [18]They make proud and stupid statements, and use immoral bodily lusts to trap those who are just beginning to escape from among people who live in error. [19]They promise them freedom, while they themselves are slaves of destructive habits—for a man is a slave of anything that has conquered him. [20]If men have escaped from the corrupting

forces of the world through their knowledge of our Lord and Saviour Jesus Christ, and then are again caught and conquered by them, such men are in worse condition at the end than they were at the beginning. ²¹It would have been much better for them never to have known the way of righteousness than to know it and then turn away from the sacred command that was given them. ²²What happened to them shows that the proverb is true, "A dog goes back to what it has vomited," and, "A pig that has been washed goes back to roll in the mud."

The proverb is true

The Promise of the Lord's Coming

3 My dear friends! This is now the second letter I have written you. In both letters I have tried to arouse pure thoughts in your minds by reminding you of these things. ²I want you to remember the words that were spoken long ago by the holy prophets, and the command from the Lord and Saviour which was given you by your apostles. ³First of all, you must understand that in the last days some men will appear whose lives are controlled by their own lusts. They will make fun of you ⁴and say, "He promised to come, didn't he? Where is he? Our fathers have already died, but everything is still the same as it was since the creation of the world!" ⁵They purposely ignore the fact that long ago God spoke, and the heavens and earth were created. The earth was formed out of water, and by water, ⁶and it was by water also, the water of the Flood, that the old world was destroyed. ⁷But the heavens and earth that now exist are being preserved, by the same word of God, for

destruction by fire. They are being kept for the day when godless men will be judged and destroyed.

8 But do not forget this one thing, my dear friends! There is no difference in the Lord's sight between one day and a thousand years; to him the two are the same. 9 The Lord is not slow to do what he has promised, as some think. Instead, he is patient with you, because he does not want anyone to be destroyed, but wants all to turn away from their sins.

10 But the Day of the Lord will come as a thief. On that Day the heavens will disappear with a shrill noise, the heavenly bodies will burn up and be destroyed, and the earth with everything in it will vanish. 11 Since all these things will be destroyed in this way, what kind of people should you be? Your lives should be holy and dedicated to God, 12 as you wait for the Day of God, and do your best to make it come soon—the Day when the heavens will burn up and be destroyed, and the heavenly bodies will be melted by the heat. 13 But we wait for what God has promised: new heavens and a new earth, where righteousness will be at home.

14 And so, my friends, as you wait for that Day, do your best to be pure and faultless in God's sight and to be at peace with him. 15 Look on our Lord's patience as the opportunity he gives you to be saved, just as our dear brother Paul wrote to you, using the wisdom God gave him. 16 This is what he says in all his letters, when he writes on this subject. There are some difficult things in his letters which ignorant and unstable people explain falsely, as they do with other passages of the Scriptures. So they bring on their own destruction.

17 But you, my friends, already know this. Be on your guard, then, so that you will not be led away by the errors of lawless men and fall from your safe position. 18 But continue to grow in the grace and knowledge of our Lord and Saviour Jesus Christ. To him be the glory, now and forever! Amen.

THE FIRST LETTER OF JOHN

The Word of Life

1 We write to you about the Word of life, which has existed from the very beginning: we have heard it, and we have seen it with our eyes; yes, we have seen it, and our hands have touched it. ²When this life became visible, we saw it; so we speak of it and tell you about the eternal life which was with the Father and was made known to us. ³What we have seen and heard we tell to you also, so that you will join with us in the fellowship that we have with the Father and with his Son Jesus Christ. ⁴We write this in order that our joy may be complete.

God Is Light

⁵Now this is the message that we have heard from his Son and announce to you: God is light and there is no darkness at all in him. ⁶If, then, we say that we have fellowship with him, yet at the same time live in the darkness, we are lying both in our words and in our actions. ⁷But if we live in the light—just as he is in the light—then we have fellowship with one another, and the blood of Jesus, his Son, makes us clean from every sin.

⁸If we say that we have no sin, we deceive ourselves and there is no truth in us. ⁹But if we confess our sins to God, he will keep his promise and do what is right: he will forgive us our sins and make us clean from all our wrongdoing. ¹⁰If we say that we have not sinned, we make a liar out of God, and his word is not in us.

Christ Our Helper

2 I write you this, my children, so that you will not sin; but if anyone does sin, we have Jesus Christ, the righteous, who pleads for us with the Father. ²And Christ himself is the means by which our sins are forgiven, and not our sins only, but also the sins of all men.

³If we obey God's commands, then we are sure that we know him. ⁴If someone says, "I do know him," but

does not obey his commands, such a person is a liar and there is no truth in him. ⁵But whoever obeys his word is the one whose love for God has really been made perfect. This is how we can be sure that we live in God: ⁶whoever says that he lives in God should live just as Jesus Christ did.

The New Command

⁷My dear friends, this command I write you is not new; it is the old command, the one you have had from the very beginning. The old command is the message you have already heard. ⁸However, the command I write you is new, and its truth is seen in Christ and also in you. For the darkness is passing away, and the real light is already shining.

⁹Whoever says that he is in the light, yet hates his brother, is in the darkness to this very hour. ¹⁰Whoever loves his brother stays in the light, and so there is nothing in him that will cause someone else to sin. ¹¹But whoever hates his brother is in the darkness; he walks in it and does not know where he is going, because the darkness has made him blind.

Whoever loves his brother stays in the light

¹²I write to you, my children, because your sins are forgiven for the sake of Christ's name. ¹³I write to you, fathers, because you know him who has existed from the beginning. I write to you, young men, because you have defeated the Evil One.

¹⁴I write to you, children, because you know the Father. I write to you, fathers, because you know him who has existed from the beginning. I write to you,

young men, because you are strong; the word of God lives in you and you have defeated the Evil One.

¹⁵Do not love the world or anything that belongs to the world. If you love the world, you do not have the love for the Father in you. ¹⁶Everything that belongs to the world—what the sinful self desires, what people see and want, and everything in this world that people are so proud of—none of this comes from the Father; it all comes from the world. ¹⁷The world and everything in it that men desire is passing away; but he who does what God wants lives forever.

The Enemy of Christ

¹⁸My children, the end is near! You were told that the Enemy of Christ would come; and now many enemies of Christ have already appeared, and so we know that the end is near. ¹⁹These people really did not belong to our group, and that is why they left us; if they had belonged to our group, they would have stayed with us. But they left so that it might be clear that none of them really belonged to our group.

²⁰But you have had the Holy Spirit poured out on you by Christ, and so all of you know the truth. ²¹I write you, then, not because you do not know the truth; instead, it is because you do know it, and also know that no lie ever comes from the truth.

²²Who, then, is the liar? It is he who says that Jesus is not the Christ. This one is the Enemy of Christ—he rejects both the Father and the Son. ²³For whoever rejects the Son also rejects the Father; whoever accepts the Son has the Father also.

²⁴Be sure, then, to keep in your hearts the message you heard from the beginning. If you keep what you heard from the beginning, then you will always live in union with the Son and the Father. ²⁵And this is what Christ himself promised to give us—eternal life.

²⁶I write you this about those who are trying to deceive you. ²⁷But as for you, Christ has poured out his Spirit on you. As long as his Spirit remains in you, you do not need anyone to teach you. For his Spirit teaches you about everything, and what he teaches is true, not

false. Obey the Spirit's teaching, then, and remain in Christ.

²⁸Yes, my children, remain in him, so that we may be full of courage when he appears and need not hide in shame from him on the Day he comes. ²⁹You know that Christ is righteous; you should know, then, that everyone who does what is right is God's child.

Children of God

3 See how much the Father has loved us! His love is so great that we are called God's children—and so, in fact, we are. This is why the world does not know us: it has not known God. ²My dear friends, we are now God's children, but it is not yet clear what we shall become. But we know that when Christ appears, we shall become like him, because we shall see him as he really is. ³Everyone who has this hope in Christ keeps himself pure, just as Christ is pure.

⁴Whoever sins is guilty of breaking God's law; because sin is a breaking of the law. ⁵You know that Christ appeared in order to take away men's sins, and that there is no sin in him. ⁶So everyone who lives in Christ does not continue to sin; but whoever continues to sin has never seen him or known him.

⁷Let no one deceive you, children! Whoever does what is right is righteous, just as Christ is righteous. ⁸Whoever continues to sin belongs to the Devil, because the Devil has sinned from the very beginning. The Son of God appeared for this very reason, to destroy the Devil's works.

⁹Whoever is a child of God does not continue to sin, because God's very nature is in him; and because God is his Father, he cannot continue to sin. ¹⁰Here is the clear difference between God's children and the Devil's children: anyone who does not do what is right, or does not love his brother, is not God's child.

Love One Another

¹¹The message you heard from the very beginning is this: we must love one another. ¹²We must not be like Cain; he belonged to the Evil One, and murdered his own brother. Why did Cain murder him? Because the

things he did were wrong, but the things his brother did were right.

[13]So do not be surprised, my brothers, if the people of the world hate you. [14]We know that we have left death and come over into life; we know it because we love our brothers. Whoever does not love is still in death. [15]Whoever hates his brother is a murderer; and you know that a murderer does not have eternal life in him. [16]This is how we know what love is: Christ gave his life for us. We too, then, ought to give our lives for our brothers! [17]If a man is rich and sees his brother in need, yet closes his heart against his brother, how can he claim that he has love for God in his heart? [18]My children! Our love should not be just words and talk; it must be true love, which shows itself in action.

Courage before God

[19]This, then, is how we will know that we belong to the truth. This is how our hearts will be confident in God's presence. [20]If our heart condemns us, we know that God is greater than our heart, and that he knows everything. [21]And so, my dear friends, if our heart does not condemn us, we have courage in God's presence. [22]We receive from him whatever we ask, because we obey his commands and do what pleases him. [23]This is what he commands: that we believe in the name of his Son Jesus Christ and love one another, just as Christ commanded us. [24]Whoever obeys God's commands lives in God and God lives in him. And this is how we know that God lives in us: we know it because of the Spirit he has given us.

The True and the False Spirit

4 My dear friends: do not believe all who claim to have the Spirit, but test them to find out if the spirit they have comes from God. For many false prophets have gone out everywhere. [2]This is how you will be able to know whether it is God's Spirit: anyone who declares that Jesus Christ came as a human being has the Spirit who comes from God. [3]But anyone who denies this about Jesus does not have the Spirit from God. This

spirit is from the Enemy of Christ; you heard that it would come, and now it is here in the world already.

⁴But you belong to God, my children, and have defeated the false prophets; because the Spirit who is in you is more powerful than the spirit in those who belong to the world. ⁵They speak about matters of the world and the world listens to them because they belong to the world. ⁶But we belong to God. Whoever knows God listens to us; whoever does not belong to God does not listen to us. This is the way, then, that we can tell the difference between the Spirit of truth and the spirit of error.

God Is Love

⁷Dear friends! Let us love one another, because love comes from God. Whoever loves is a child of God and knows God. ⁸Whoever does not love does not know God, because God is love. ⁹This is how God showed his love for us: he sent his only Son into the world that we might have life through him. ¹⁰This is what love is: it is not that we have loved God, but that he loved us and sent his Son to be the means by which our sins are forgiven.

¹¹Dear friends, if this is how God loved us, then we should love one another. ¹²No one has ever seen God; if we love one another, God lives in us and his love is made perfect in us.

¹³This is how we are sure that we live in God and he lives in us: he has given us his Spirit. ¹⁴And we have seen and tell others that the Father sent his Son to be the Saviour of the world. ¹⁵Whoever declares that Jesus is the Son of God, God lives in him, and he lives in God. ¹⁶And we ourselves know and believe the love which God has for us.

God is love, and whoever lives in love lives in God and God lives in him. ¹⁷The purpose of love being made perfect in us is that we may have courage on Judgment Day; and we will have it because our life in this world is the same as Christ's. ¹⁸There is no fear in love; perfect love drives out all fear. So then, love has not been made perfect in the one who fears, because fear has to do with punishment.

Perfect love drives out all fear

¹⁹We love because God first loved us. ²⁰If someone says, "I love God," but hates his brother, he is a liar. For he cannot love God, whom he has not seen, if he does not love his brother, whom he has seen. ²¹This, then, is the command that Christ gave us: he who loves God must love his brother also.

Our Victory over the World

5 Whoever believes that Jesus is the Messiah is a child of God; and whoever loves a father loves his child also. ²This is how we know that we love God's children: it is by loving God and obeying his commands. ³For our love for God means that we obey his commands. And his commands are not too hard for us, ⁴because every child of God is able to defeat the world. This is how we win the victory over the world: with our faith. ⁵Who can defeat the world? Only he who believes that Jesus is the Son of God.

The Witness about Jesus Christ

⁶Jesus Christ is the one who came; he came with the water of his baptism and the blood of his death. He came not only with the water, but with both the water and the blood. And the Spirit himself testifies that this is true, because the Spirit is truth. ⁷There are three witnesses,

⁸the Spirit, the water, and the blood; and all three agree.
⁹We believe the witness that men give; the witness that
God gives is much stronger, and this is the witness that
God has given about his Son. ¹⁰So whoever believes in
the Son of God has this witness in his heart; but whoever
does not believe God has made a liar out of him, because
he has not believed what God has said as a witness about
his Son. ¹¹This, then, is the witness: God has given us
eternal life, and this life is in his Son. ¹²Whoever has the
Son has this life; whoever does not have the Son of God
does not have life.

Keep yourselves safe from false gods

Eternal Life

¹³I write you this so that you may know that you have
eternal life—you that believe in the name of the Son of
God. ¹⁴We have courage in God's presence because we
are sure that he hears us if we ask him for anything that
is according to his will. ¹⁵He hears us whenever we ask
him; since we know this is true, we know also that he
gives us what we ask from him.

¹⁶If anyone sees his brother commit a sin that does not
lead to death, he should pray to God, who will give him
life. This applies to those whose sins do not lead to
death. But there is sin which leads to death, and I do not
say that you should pray to God about that. ¹⁷All wrongdoing is sin, but there is sin which does not lead to
death.

¹⁸We know that no child of God keeps on sinning,
because the Son of God keeps him safe, and the Evil
One cannot harm him.

[19]We know that we belong to God even though the whole world is under the rule of the Evil One.

[20]We know that the Son of God has come and has given us understanding, so that we know the true God. Our lives are in the true God—in his Son Jesus Christ. This is the true God, and this is eternal life.

[21]My children, keep yourselves safe from false gods!

THE SECOND LETTER OF JOHN

[1]From the Elder—

To the dear Lady and to her children, whom I truly love. I am not the only one, but all who know the truth love you, [2]because the truth remains in us and will be with us forever.

[3]May God the Father and Jesus Christ, the Father's Son, give us grace, mercy, and peace; may they be ours in truth and love.

Truth and Love

[4]How happy I was to find that some of your children live in the truth, just as the Father commanded us. [5]And so I ask you, dear Lady: let us all love one another. This is no new command I write you; it is the command which we have had from the beginning. [6]This love I speak of means that we must live in obedience to God's commands. The command, as you have all heard from the beginning, is this: you must all live in love.

[7]Many deceivers have gone out over the world, men who do not declare that Jesus Christ came as a human being. Such a person is a deceiver and the Enemy of Christ. [8]Watch yourselves, then, so that you will not lose what you have worked for, but will receive your reward in full.

[9]Anyone who does not stay with the teaching of Christ, but goes beyond it, does not have God. Whoever does stay with the teaching has both the Father and the Son. [10]If anyone comes to you, then, who does not bring this teaching, do not welcome him in your home; do not even say, "Peace be with you." [11]For anyone who wishes him peace becomes his partner in the evil things he does.

Final Words

[12]I have so much to tell you, but I would rather not do it with paper and ink; instead, I hope to visit you and talk with you personally, so that we shall be completely happy.

[13]The children of your dear Sister send you their greetings.

THE THIRD LETTER OF JOHN

[1]From the Elder—
To my dear Gaius, whom I truly love.
[2]My dear friend, I pray that everything may go well with you, and that you may be in good health—as I know you are well in spirit. [3]I was so happy when some brothers arrived and told how faithful you are to the truth—just as you always live in the truth. [4]Nothing makes me happier than to hear that my children live in the truth.

Gaius Is Praised

[5]My dear friend, you are so faithful in the work you do for the brothers, even when they are strangers. [6]They have spoken of your love to the church here. Please help them to continue their journey in a way that will please God. [7]For they set out on their journey in the service of Christ without accepting any help from unbelievers. [8]We Christians, then, must help these men, so that we may share in their work for the truth.

Diotrephes and Demetrius

[9]I wrote a short letter to the church; but Diotrephes, who loves to be their leader, will not pay any attention to what I say. [10]When I come, then, I will bring up everything he has done: the terrible things he says about us and the lies he tells! But that is not enough for him; he will not receive the brothers when they come, and even stops those who want to receive them and tries to drive them out of the church!

[11]My dear friend, do not imitate what is bad, but imitate what is good. Whoever does good belongs to God; whoever does what is bad has not seen God.

[12]Everyone speaks well of Demetrius; truth itself speaks well of him. And we add our witness, and you know that what we say is true.

Final Greetings

[13]I have so much to tell you, but I do not want to do it with pen and ink. [14]I hope to see you soon, and then we will talk personally.

[15]Peace be with you.

All your friends send greetings. Greet all our friends personally.

THE LETTER FROM JUDE

[1]From Jude, a servant of Jesus Christ, and the brother of James—

To those who have been called by God, who live in the love of God the Father and the protection of Jesus Christ:

[2]May mercy, peace, and love be yours in full measure.

False Teachers

[3]My dear friends! I was doing my best to write to you about the salvation we share in common, when I felt the need of writing you now to encourage you to fight on for the faith which once and for all God has given to his people. [4]For some godless men have slipped in unnoticed among us, who distort the message about the grace of our God to excuse their immoral ways, and reject Jesus Christ, our only Master and Lord. Long ago the Scriptures predicted this condemnation they have received.

[5]For even though you know all this, I want to remind you of how the Lord saved the people of Israel from the land of Egypt, but afterwards destroyed those who did not believe. [6]Remember the angels who did not stay within the limits of their proper authority, but abandoned their own dwelling place: they are bound with eternal chains in the darkness below, where God is keeping them for that great Day on which they will be condemned. [7]Remember Sodom and Gomorrah, and the nearby towns, whose people acted as those angels did and committed sexual immorality and perversion: they suffer the punishment of eternal fire as a plain warning to all.

[8]In the same way also, these men have visions which make them sin against their own bodies; they despise God's authority and insult the glorious beings above. [9]Not even the chief angel Michael has done this. In his quarrel with the Devil, when they argued about who would have the body of Moses, Michael did not dare condemn the Devil with insulting words, but said, "The

Lord rebuke you!" [10]But these men insult things they do not understand; and those things that they know by instinct, like wild animals, are the very things that destroy them. [11]How terrible for them! They have followed the way that Cain took. For the sake of money they have given themselves over to the error that Balaam committed. They have rebelled as Korah rebelled, and like him they are destroyed. [12]They are like dirty spots in your fellowship meals, with their shameless carousing. They take care of themselves only. They are like clouds carried along by the wind and bringing no rain. They are like trees that bear no fruit, even in autumn, trees that have been pulled up by the roots and are completely dead. [13]They are like wild waves of the sea, with their shameful deeds showing up like foam. They are like wandering stars, for whom God has reserved a place forever in the deepest darkness.

[14]It was Enoch, the sixth direct descendant from Adam, who long ago prophesied this about them: "Look! The Lord will come with many thousands of his holy angels, [15]to bring judgment on all, to condemn all godless sinners for all the godless deeds they have performed, and for all the terrible words these godless men have spoken against God!"

[16]These men are always grumbling and blaming others; they follow their own evil desires; they brag about themselves, and flatter others in order to get their own way.

Warnings and Instructions

[17]But remember, my friends! Remember what you were told in the past by the apostles of our Lord Jesus Christ. [18]They said to you, "When the last days come, men will appear who will make fun of you, men who follow their own godless desires." [19]These are the men who cause divisions, who are controlled by their natural desires, who do not have the Spirit. [20]But you, my friends, keep on building yourselves up on your most sacred faith. Pray in the power of the Holy Spirit, [21]and keep yourselves in the love of God, as you wait for our Lord Jesus Christ in his mercy to give you eternal life.

²²Show mercy towards those who have doubts: ²³save them, by snatching them out of the fire. Show mercy also, mixed with fear, to others as well, but hate their very clothes, stained by their sinful lusts.

Prayer of Praise

²⁴To him who is able to keep you from falling and bring you faultless and joyful before his glorious presence—²⁵to the only God our Saviour, through Jesus Christ our Lord, be glory, majesty, might, and authority, from all ages past, and now, and forever and ever! Amen.

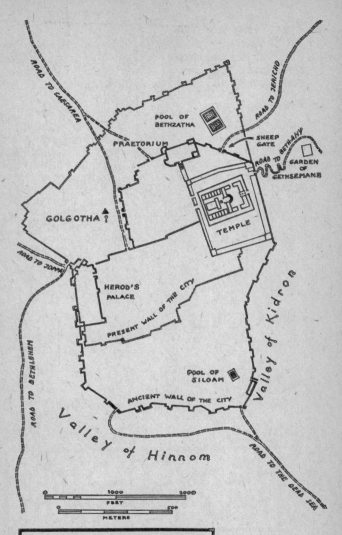

JERUSALEM
and its surroundings

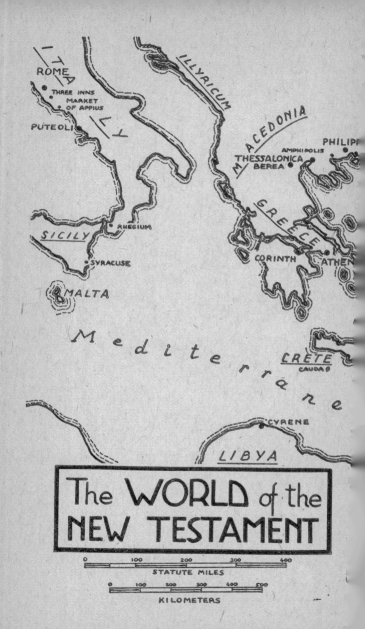

The WORLD of the NEW TESTAMENT

Good News for Modern Man

The New Testament: Today's English Version

'I commend this version . . . an outstanding addition to the Fontana Religious Series.'
Archbishop of York

'TEV with its scrupulous accuracy and fresh contemporary language makes a valuable contribution to a better understanding of God's revealed Word. It will be helpful in particular to all those who are engaged in the pursuit of the two principal ecumenical aims of twentieth-century Christianity: renewal and reunion. I am grateful to Collins Publishers for including TEV in its Religious Fontana Series and wish it every best success.'
Archbishop H. E. Cardinale, Apostolic Delegate to Great Britain

'As new as the new year the British paperback edition of the New Testament Today's English Version GOOD NEWS FOR MODERN MAN will in the coming weeks be catching the public eye on bookshop counters, at street-corner, railway and airport bookstalls, in tobacconists, general stores, and supermarkets. The Good News will be where the people go.'
Methodist Recorder

Good News for Modern Man

Editions available in the United Kingdom published by Collins Fontana Books

Sing a New Song
  (The Psalms in Today's English Version)

Good News for Modern Man
  (The New Testament in Today's English Version)

3rd edition
Available in hardback

Published jointly by the British and Foreign Bible Society and the National Bible Society of Scotland in association with Collins Fontana Books.

New Testament illustrated paperback

New Testament paperback without illustrations

Single books with illustrations

Matthew	80 pages
Mark	64 pages
Luke	84 pages
John	64 pages
Philippians	16 pages

Each Gospel available in large type

THE BIBLE READING FELLOWSHIP

Readers of this commentary may wish to follow a regular pattern of Bible reading, designed to cover the Bible roughly on the basis of a book a month. Suitable Notes (send for details) with helpful exposition and prayers are provided by the Bible Reading Fellowship three times a year (January to April, May to August, September to December), and are available from:—

UK
The Bible Reading Fellowship,
St Michael's House,
2 Elizabeth Street,
London, SW1W 9RQ

USA
The Bible Reading Fellowship,
P.O. Box 299, Winter Park,
Florida 32789, USA.

AUSTRALIA
The Bible Reading Fellowship,
Jamieson House,
Constitution Avenue, Reid,
Canberra, ACT 2601,
Australia.